ANGELS KEEP WATCH

ANGELS KEEP WATCH

Carol Hathorne

CHIVERS LARGE PRINT
BATH

This Large Print edition published by BBC Audiobooks, Bath, 2003.
Published by arrangement with the author.

U.K. Hardcover ISBN 0 7540 7220 7
U.K. Softcover ISBN 0 7540 7221 5

Printed and bound in Great Britain by
Antony Rowe Ltd., Chippenham, Wiltshire

To Ancrum, with thanks.

'See that you don't despise any of these little ones. Their angels in heaven, I tell you, are always in the presence of my Father in heaven.'

Matthew 18:10 (Good News Bible).

CONTENTS

CHAPTER ONE

It is 1954. I am ten years old. I am sitting on my bed and a voice inside me says, 'Go to Africa.'

Africa is really just a word. A map which I cut out of some leaflet I was given at Sunday school. I'm writing a book about Africa, and on page one there is another cut-out picture—Jesus Christ on the cross. It is because of him, and knowing he is in my heart for ever that I have to go to Africa. Even at this young age, I feel sure that there I will share him more fully with those who really understand.

My fascination—vocation, if you like—is almost mystical. Disturbing and scary, it's such a contrast to the real world around me. My grandmother is in that world. In some ways she's the centre of it. With time to be interested in me, she sits in her council house in the Black Country industrial town of Tipton. She sews and knits and tells stories which I devour as greedily as I do her delicious egg custard and spicy bread puddings.

At home, another council house less than a mile away, there's always hassle. My mother is thin and dangerous, her grim pride propelling her as she fetches the pensions and boils the white bloomers of her own grandmother and aunt. Both of them live with us, and at night I

1

lie awake in the box room I share with my brother and listen to them slandering her.

'Er as we money, yer know! When er's bin to the post office!'

'Ar, an' er's on'y the lodger!'

We are all 'lodgers', I vaguely understand from overhearing my mother talking to the next-door neighbour (another aunt) because the old lady's name is in the rent book. At ten, none of it really makes sense to me, except that at times I feel like baby Jesus for whom there was no room at the inn.

The night the old lady dies I lie in bed, transfixed, listening to the angels singing. I've tried so hard to keep my brother awake, going round to his side of the bed, shaking him and talking to him. I'm convinced we have been left in the house alone with the corpse, though reason now tells me this could not have been so.

The moonlight pours in through the cotton curtain across the window which, although identical to every other in the street, is different being ours. I am cold and scared, more lonely than I knew was possible, even though my brother sleeps nearby. I look at the shrine I have made in 'my corner', with my Bible and Sunday school star card, and my writing book about Africa. My life is an ongoing conversation with God, and I pray and pray.

I think of the old lady, so different to my

indulgent nan, and remember how, only a few days ago, encouraged by my mother, I knitted garters for her to hold her stockings up. She had put them on in bed, tugging the baggy lisle stockings up over her wasted, ninety-two-year-old legs while I stared, repelled and fascinated. She had paid me twopence and, flushed with success and affluence, I had wondered briefly if perhaps Aunt Maud would like some knitted garters too?

It's as the thought and the prayer fuse together that the angel voices come. Far away and yet near, wafting in on the air of that clear night before the factory 'bulls' blow out their signal to pollute the sky. I catch my breath and jumping up again, dig my fingers into my sleeping brother's arm. But only I can hear the singing. At least, that's what I think until the next morning. When I get up and go downstairs, I hear my mother telling the next-door aunt: 'I know Gran's all right. Last night I heard the angels singing.'

*   *   *

It is 1995. Fifty-one years old, I wake in the room I share with my Methodist minister husband, and a voice inside me says, 'Go to Africa.'

I have heard it many times over the past forty-one years, though not at regular or even vaguely explicable intervals. As a library

3

assistant, fresh out of school, I chose books about Africa for my father who was strangely fascinated by the black (mostly West Indian) immigrants who were flooding into Britain at that time. When race riots flared in Dudley he was there, standing firmly side by side with the immigrants, our large Alsatian dog beside him. Taking the books home for him reminded me of when I had imagined myself a missionary. That pious little girl was scarcely more than a memory now. Even in my wildest dreams I couldn't imagine her coming back to life.

Much later, I encountered Africa again at second or even third hand. An old lady I knew had relatives 'at the Cape'. She talked about their life there, and of her own delight in experiencing the breath-taking scenery and luxurious life-style when visiting them. In those days, apartheid was enforced in South Africa, and I firmly shut my ears to her eulogy. The muffled voice of God, meanwhile, spoke again as I wandered around supermarkets and fruit stalls, earnestly boycotting any item that carried a South-African sticker.

My call into ministry then took precedence. For a long time, through selection, training, ordination to the diaconate and then the priesthood, I felt I could breathe a sigh of relief and forget about Africa. The voice I had heard, the strange, inexplicable stirrings could be explained after all: I had a vocation which would be fulfilled through my local, busy experience of priesthood.

And so it was for a long time. Except that while in training college, I was chosen to be the Link person for CMS (Church Missionary Society) missionaries—in Africa. As I wrote to them I couldn't help but wonder. What was it like on that vast continent? And why was God still determined to keep me wondering about it? I resolved to throw myself instead into being a missionary in the Black Country, where I had been born. This came so naturally that I could scarcely believe it when, some five years later, I began to hear again that still, small voice saying, 'Go to Africa.'

I jump out of bed and, even before I get dressed, I say silently but pragmatically, 'Right, Lord, if you really want me to go to Africa, the prayers today will be for Africa.'

'That'll stop him!' I think foolishly, as I put on my cassock and cross the road for church. 'It'll be a relief not to hear that voice and have that uncomfortable niggle again. Better still, I'll be able to get on with my life and ministry.'

Ten minutes later, I'm hearing my unsuspecting colleague read calmly from the Anglican Cycle of Prayer: 'We pray today for the continent of Africa.' I stumble home, dazed and bewildered, knowing the laugh is on me, to share it with my husband Mark.

CHAPTER TWO

'OK, let's go one step further,' Mark suggested as I finished my rather garbled account. So in our prayers that day, we decided to ask for a sign from God.

'Lord, we don't know anybody even remotely connected with Africa! If you want us to go, you'll have to make it possible!' we said.

In the very ordinary living room of our Methodist manse, with the gas fire popping and the noise of the traffic on the road outside, it seemed such an outlandish request. We looked at each other, smiled and almost shrugged.

Nothing would happen. How could it? And yet . . .

It is a fearful thing to fall into the hands of the living God. I had no inkling whatsoever that the trap was not only set, waiting to catch me, but nicely baited too.

It happened that one Friday evening in late October I had been invited to preach at a harvest festival at the tiny church of St Bartholomew's, Lower Sapey, a village set in the heart of agricultural Worcestershire, and about as different to the Black Country as you can get. Sheep grazed on the gently rolling hills and the church was hidden away, barely accessible by lanes overgrown with hedgerows and scarcely wide enough for a single car.

My sermon was about harvest in the Black Country, illustrated by a carrier bag full of litter papers and empty drinks cans that seemed to demonstrate very well our two different worlds. I had no idea that yet another world—for me a very significant one—was about to explode into being almost before my eyes. All I remember is that before the service the Methodist local preacher, who was in the vestry with me, mentioned that St Bartholomew's had a mission link—with a hospital in Kenya.

I listened to some of the details. The parish had been raising funds for the hospital, which had a charitable scheme called the Samaritan fund to pay for destitute patients. The rector himself had recently undergone a bicycle ride from John o'Groats to Lands End in order to raise funds. Then, while an absurd bell rang in my astonished ears, I heard myself say, 'That's funny. I've always felt the Lord is calling me to go to Africa.'

The man responded as if my comment were the most natural thing in the world. 'You should talk to Ancrum Evans then, our patron,' he suggested. 'He's the major shareholder in the hospital. He might be able to arrange for you to go over there.'

'No way!' I didn't say the words aloud, but that was my unworthy, instinctive reaction! After the service, as we all trooped across the

7

pitch-black leafy lane for the harvest supper in the church hall, I whispered urgently to Mark, 'It's an amazing coincidence, after our prayers. But, well, I'm not going to mention it to this man!'

Altogether, Africa was getting much too close for comfort. So I concentrated on making small talk with the Lower Sapey congregation, and enjoying a delicious ploughman's supper followed by apple pie and cream. When the patron, the blunt but personable Mr Evans was introduced to me, I just smiled politely and tried to forget what I had heard about his foreign connections. He looked straight at me. 'What are your future plans?' he asked. A question which, looking back, I don't remember being asked very often during my lifetime. I again heard the 'bell' and remembered that age-old, tireless request from within me. 'Well,' I stammered, 'I've always thought the Lord is calling me to go to Africa.'

There, it was out! There had been no flash of lightning, no thunderbolt. Mr Evans would probably shrug and ask another question, or maybe turn and talk to someone else. Now I had said it, I could forget it again.

Ancrum Evans frowned, obviously taken aback. 'What do you know about Africa?' he asked challengingly.

'Nothing.' As I made this shamefaced admission, he fixed me with an unwavering look in which for one split second I seemed to catch a reflection of my own fascination with a far-off land. He explained quickly that he had been in Kenya during the second world war and had developed lasting bonds with the East Africans. His business interests there had been frozen on independence and, seeing the desperate need for health care, he had invested in a hospital to be managed and staffed by Kenyans.

'If you really feel called to Africa, it might be an idea to find out why,' he said. 'I'll be in Nairobi next week for the official opening of the hospital. Send me your CVs and I'll see what I can do.'

Still I clung onto the edges of my pool of security, afraid to let the waves carry me out on God's tide. On the way home I talked with Mark, and we agreed again that all this was strange. But we didn't know the first thing about our benefactor, and we were strangers to him. What possible use could our CVs be in his concerns at this Nairobi hospital, especially as neither of us had any medical experience?

On the Monday afternoon, there was a message on our answerphone. Mr Ancrum Evans had felt compelled to ascertain our phone number from the bicycling rector who had engaged me to preach. If I were really serious about going to Africa, he repeated, we must send our CVs immediately. He would then try and arrange for us to go to Kenya to,

9

as he put it, 'explore the call'.

'Well, we asked the Lord to make it possible,' Mark reminded me, as we sat together at the word processor that evening. 'We can't complain if he does!'

It could still come to nothing, I half hoped, giving way to the uncertainty still washing round my whitened knuckles. Why should anyone in Nairobi want two inexperienced English clergy foisted on them? Ancrum Evans was obviously a well-meaning but impractical optimist.

Three weeks later, on Friday 3rd November, we received a letter from him, posted from his estate office in Lower Sapey after being faxed from Buruburu, Nairobi. 'All systems GO!' it began.

CHAPTER THREE

The plan was that we should initially spend three months in Kenya, from April to June 1996. We would live as Africans on the eastern side of the city of Nairobi, and work in the churches. Our brief as far as Ancrum was concerned was to help raise the profile of the Metropolitan Hospital. We would do this by encouraging a chaplaincy link with the local clergy and by advertising the Samaritan fund, a trust scheme by which those unable to afford

10

medical treatment might obtain it at the hospital through the Christian charity of other stockholders.

'I will arrange accommodation, plus a cook and driver, as it will not be safe for you to drive yourselves,' our amazing benefactor said. 'I will guarantee your air fares, though you will obviously have to supply your own living expenses.'

He added a postscript that brought another unexpected tinkle to the bell at the back of my mind: 'I personally have never experienced anything like what is happening to me now.'

'He means the Holy Spirit,' I said as Mark and I looked at each other, still trying to take it all in. 'It sounds great, but how can we just leave the house, the family, even the dog and cat, for three whole months?'

'We could ask Liz,' Mark suggested. 'She never minds taking care of things when we go on holiday.'

'I'll ring her.' Already I was drawing up a list in my head. 'But first, why don't you make some inquiries about taking a sabbatical. You're due for one.'

During twenty years in American and British Methodism, Mark had never applied for sabbatical leave, and could now officially do so. My own non-stipendiary position with the Church of England was rather more fluid, although I would have to clear things with my vicar and the parochial church council before I

11

could disappear for three months.

We were half way through the necessary formal telephone calls when the telephone rang. I couldn't believe my ears when a voice I hadn't heard for ages said: 'Hi, Caz. It's Liz!'

'But I was going to ring *you*!' I gabbled, nodding to the grinning Mark. 'Oh Liz, you'll never guess what's happened!'

Scarcely daring to hope, I explained about the chance to go to Africa, and how it all depended on her willingness and availability to stay at the manse. The snag was that this was not for a couple of weeks, as on previous occasions, but for three whole months!

To my surprise and delight, Liz did not hesitate. 'I'll come,' she said decisively. 'Don't worry. We'll work out the details later. You just carry on with your arrangements.'

She was, she told us later, certain even then that it was the Lord's will for us to go, and for her to help make it possible.

By the end of November, all our Methodist and Anglican congregations knew we were going to Africa. The reaction was mixed. Some people imagined wildlife safaris and white sands, and congratulated us on having the chance to take such a long exotic holiday. Others, bothered by images from old movies, joked half seriously about missionaries and cooking pots. To us, with Christmas and then Easter services to get through before we left, it all seemed rather like a dream. If we didn't think about it, it wasn't going to happen.

Anxious moments came and went. I worried about breaking the news to our married daughter, Sarah, from whom I had never been apart for three months before. Her reaction, disconcerting but consoling, was: 'Can I use the car while you're away?'

Mark was concerned about seventeen-year-old Edmund who would be sitting his vital A levels while we were away. Would he feel rejected and emotionally bereft and show it by throwing wild parties the minute our backs were turned?

I also worried about our pets, Becky the dog and Jacob the cat. Lying awake with loyal Becky under the bed, and the blue-eyed Siamese on my chest, I imagined a kind of 'Incredible Journey' scenario, with the two of them desperately setting out to look for their errant owners. And never being seen again.

'Why, Lord?' I asked, when I looked at the local Sunday school I had worked so hard to start, the dance worship class that was going from strength to strength. 'Why do you want us to leave everything in mid air and go off to Africa?'

'We only know he does,' Mark pointed out, reminding me of our prayers of acceptance and the coincidences which had followed. 'How much more proof do you need?'

Obviously just a tiny bit more, the Lord must have decided. For one day, at the beginning of December, Ancrum Evans decided to visit the Black Country to see us, and to talk to my parish church council about the trip to Kenya.

The meeting was planned for the Tuesday evening, and Ancrum was due to come to the manse in the afternoon and eat with us beforehand. On the Tuesday morning, Mark and I went over to St Mark's as usual for Morning Prayer. It was my turn to lead it, and when the time came for prayers, I opened the Anglican Cycle of Prayer. Automatically breathing a sigh of relief when I saw that this week's prayers were all for the United States of America, I looked down the list and found Tuesday 12th December. 'Kenya Independence Day' it said in bold black print. 'Please pray for Kenya.'

CHAPTER FOUR

At just after 7 am on a Wednesday morning in April, Nairobi airport was almost deserted. With the other passengers from our Air Kenya flight from Heathrow, we formed a queue at the admissions desk, trying to ignore the fact that no one was actually working behind it.

Suddenly, a rather tired-looking large African man appeared and took up a position behind another desk, motioning us all unhurriedly to move over. Over that desk was a written notice: 'It is illegal to offer or accept a bribe. Please report all attempts at bribery immediately to the authorities.'

'Shades of *Nineteen Eighty Four*,' I whispered to Mark in surprise. 'What does it mean? That people give bribes to get things in or out of the country?'

'I expect so,' Mark replied as we showed our passports to the unsmiling guard. 'Remember what we've been told about corruption in high places?'

A moment later, we passed through to reclaim our luggage, and as I watched the assortment of bags and suitcases going by on the carousel, I couldn't help but think of the amazing collection of items we had brought with us. A mosquito net, of course, plus the obligatory anti-malaria drugs, water-purifying tablets, candles and matches, an electric kettle, radio, rechargeable batteries and portable charger. It had felt more like packing for a camping trip than preparing to spend three months on the outskirts of a city!

But Ancrum and other seasoned travellers we had met over the previous few months had assured us these were the things we would most need. 'You can leave most of them behind as gifts when you return to the UK,' Ancrum had consoled when we pointed out the combined weight and bulk of all this hardware. 'You'll find they're all very desirable items where you're going.'

Eventually, the four battered suitcases trundled hugely into sight, and we tugged them onto a trolley. As we pushed it rather nervously into the area where people waited, we scanned the rows of black faces, wondering how we were supposed to recognise Julius, our African driver.

In spite of myself, I remembered a story I had heard only the previous week of British tourists being kidnapped by an unscrupulous Nairobi taxi driver who proceeded to drive them up an alley and steal all their luggage, including their passports and travellers' cheques.

Again, my pitiful lack of faith was showing. Although we weren't wearing our clerical collars, as previously arranged, Julius had no trouble at all in recognising us. A tall, slender young man, he came to meet us, hand outstretched, smiling in shy greeting: 'Mark and Carol Hathorne? *Karibu*. Welcome to Nairobi!'

Mark and I exchanged a silent sigh of relief. That was the first major hurdle over. We followed the young man out of the airport into the bright heat of the day across the car park to a battered white saloon car. Deftly loading our luggage into the boot, Julius opened the doors and we were soon inside.

'I take you to the flat,' he suggested quietly. 'You must be tired.'

Strangely enough, the effects of the long flight seemed to have miraculously vanished. Besides, as the old car jerked and then began to move forward, there was altogether too much to see. The land near the airport was dusty and bare except for dwarf trees and patches of beautifully green grass, caused, so Julius said, by the rainy season. The colours of the flowering bushes we passed were beautiful, crimson, yellow and white blooms of exotic shape and size.

But the main thing that took my breath away was the vast, undulating ocean of people. There were people simply everywhere—in suits, or African dress, in school uniforms, in rags. People walking across flat open spaces or standing in untidy groups waiting for tiny, screeching, overcrowded buses. People lying flat on the ground under trees, or trying to sell dusty looking fruit and vegetables at the side of the road. Except in news pictures of places like Calcutta or Bombay I had never seen anything like it. And there wasn't a single white face anywhere!

'We go now on Jogoo Road,' Julius explained as the car bounced and skidded round a corner. As we hit an enormous pot-hole, both of us jumped about two feet into the air.

'Andy would love this!' Mark chuckled, as we both thought about our car-mad son-in-law. 'Talk about dirt-track racing!'

The unpaved road was a mass of dust and vehicles without the safety of traffic signals or, it seemed to me, even brakes! Cars, trucks, bicycles, and people, horse-like, pulling hand carts. They all went their own way, tooting to let the rest of the world know they were there, turning haphazardly into one another's paths, changing direction as the fancy took them, like dodgem cars at the fair.

Meanwhile the sights of Jogoo Road zoomed past my mesmerised eyes. Huts and shacks. Dilapidated structures that obviously passed for shops. Schools and nurseries that wouldn't have passed nineteenth-century British health legislation. Market stalls made of rocks and branches, with tatty pieces of polythene draped across them, selling everything from live chickens to second-hand clothes. Women carrying enormous bundles or baskets on their heads, or, like beasts of burden, across their shoulders, bending them double.

Near a garage and recognisable supermarket, we passed advertisement hoardings for Sloanes liniment, and Omo washing powder, and a hand-painted sign pointing in the direction of a botanical doctor. He could, it was claimed, cure anything from insanity to diarrhoea with his herbal potions.

At a dustily dangerous corner, we slowed down alongside a herd of goats, happily feasting on a smoking rubbish tip. At the same time, two minibuses appeared out of nowhere, mud splattered and dilapidated, one each side of us. As one swayed across my vision, spilling passengers and loud music as it jerked to a halt, I glimpsed the words 'God is Love' painted in red over the yellow door.

'*Matatus*,' Julius explained with a philosophical shrug, sounding his horn. 'They are a problem here.'

Only one problem, I realised, as we travelled on. Already I was speechless, every sense challenged by the sights and sounds being presented like a crazy magic lantern show before me. What on earth was coming next?

CHAPTER FIVE

Doonholm was a development area, a churned-up building site with shacks on the corner and more wandering goats. From one spot on the building site, smoke arose and huddled figures could be seen sitting on the earth around a fitful open fire. One of the first sights my dazed eyes registered was an enormous green marquee with a sign outside: 'Living Word African Gospel Church. English service 11 am. All welcome.'

The flat itself was behind an iron gate, with the faint numbers '104' painted on it, in a street without a name. Along the length of the high concrete wall adjacent to the gate was an expanse of lethal-looking broken glass. To get into the upstairs building, as Julius now demonstrated, one must pass through the gate and up a flight of stairs, first negotiating two padlocks.

'Security I suppose,' Mark said as I rather worriedly met his eyes. 'I expect they have quite a few break-ins in an area like this.'

I followed him over the threshold, through a steel door whose glass panels were protected by curved iron bars. The windows had bars too, I noticed, making entrance through them virtually impossible.

My first impressions of 104 Doonholm were of pleasant surprise, for it really was quite comfortable, with a rattan three-piece suite, television and coffee table in the sitting room. The kitchen, which we passed on our way to the bedroom with our luggage, was clean but very basic, reminding me instantly of my late grandmother's house in 1950s Britain. The shelf above the sink was lined with newspaper, and held dried food stored in thick paper bags, while on the stone floor stood a plastic container full of vegetables. The bedroom, which again had barred windows, was almost filled with a double bed, though there was a built-in wardrobe and two small items of rattan furniture which matched the sitting-room suite.

After our journey and all the excitement, all I really wanted was a cup of tea and a lie down, followed by a hot bath or shower and a change of clothes. But the bathroom leading off the bedroom didn't seem to have any recognisable facilities—just a grid in the floor, a tap in the wall, and a toilet. I contented myself with sitting in a chair and trying to sort out who was who. For I suddenly realised that the flat was full of Africans, all speaking in rapid Swahili.

'I am Rose.' An attractive young woman with a fashionable European hairstyle came in from the hall, holding out her hand. 'I am secretary at the Metropolitan Hospital. You are very welcome.'

We shook hands, and Mark and I introduced ourselves. 'We are arranging for you to have a cook as Mr Evans instructed,' Rose explained, as two other ladies, smiling, came out of the kitchen to shake hands. 'And Dr Gakombe, the hospital director, will be along to see you later. If there is anything you would like, just let us know.'

I thought longingly of the bed and the tea. But the bed was in the process of being made up, and stupid though it might sound, I wasn't even certain that they drank tea in this part of the world. Suddenly I thought about the mosquito net we had brought with us, paid for by a worried elderly lady from my congregation. 'We'd like to have a rest,' I told Rose, 'but first, we'll need to fix our mosquito net over the bed.'

As far as I could see, there were no mosquitoes in the flat. We had been told that they only came out at night. But it seemed very important that the net should be fixed before we were left alone there. It seemed to take hours to fit the net, a process which involved Julius going away and coming back again, and several more young women arriving, and the first two leaving. But eventually, hooks were screwed into the wooden ceiling and the rectangular net suspended over the double bed.

We fell onto the bed gratefully. When we awoke, some two hours later, it was to the sound of chickens clucking noisily in the yard below the window. And to the smell of something delicious drifting temptingly from the old-fashioned kitchen.

'*Jambo!*' As we stumbled back into the living room, we were greeted by a velvety faced woman in a colourful African dress. 'I am Wilomenah. I cook for you.'

Realising how long it had been since our inflight breakfast, we gave thanks and eagerly uncovered the food Wilomenah set before us. Soon we were enjoying our first sight and taste of *ugali*.

'It is made from maize flour,' Rose explained as she sat down to enjoy her own meal. 'We say in Africa it makes you strong so that you can dig ditches!'

Along with the dumpling-like *ugali*, Wilomenah had prepared chicken in a tomato-based sauce, and bright green spinach. It was followed by refreshing slices of orange paw-paw, the freshest tropical fruit I had ever tasted. After the meal, tea appeared, made with hot milk from a huge blue thermos. Though it wasn't the strong English tea we were used to, we were very grateful to see it.

While we were being so well taken care of, people continued to arrive to greet us, all of them shaking hands and saying, surprisingly, '*Bwana Asifiwe!* Praise the Lord!'

Suddenly, a car pulled up outside the gate. 'It is Dr Gakombe,' Rose said, stretching, cat like, at the window. She went over to unlock the steel door.

Kaenja Gakombe was a smartly dressed, bespectacled Kenyan in his early thirties. He entered the flat, smiling his welcome. 'We are so happy you are here,' he said. 'Is everything satisfactory?'

As we replied that things were more than satisfactory, he explained that until that morning, the hospital had been expecting us the following week!

'We received a fax from Mr Evans last night to say you were on your way,' he said with a little shrug. 'So since then we have all been busy, busy, busy!'

The activity was still going on. From the kitchen there was the sound of washing up, competing with the rise and fall of Swahili voices. Unused to being waited on, I fidgeted a little, wondering how much Wilomenah would be doing for us. However necessary, the idea of employing 'servants' felt decadently colonial, and not at all what we had travelled here for.

'I have brought you some papers,' Dr Gakombe said, placing two rather grim-looking tabloid newspapers on the coffee table. 'They will give you some idea of what life is like here in Kenya.'

After promising to look at them, we found our diaries and checked the two appointments Ancrum had made on our behalf, the first at St Stephen's church the next morning.

'Julius will collect you,' Dr Gakombe said confidently. 'But first thing, perhaps you would like to come to the hospital for a guided tour?'

'We would very much,' Mark agreed. 'And really, we should send a fax to Mr Evans to let him know we have arrived.'

Looking around, I felt my first pang of homesickness. In a rash moment I had promised Sarah a telephone call to let her know we were safe. With no telephone in the flat, and no phone boxes on the building site outside, that was obviously going to be impossible. Still, they must have telephones at the hospital. And tomorrow wasn't all that far away. I felt that way right up until the moment our last helper, Wilomenah, left. Then, as

Mark came back from locking the outer and inner gates and padlocking the front door, I looked around at the darkness, gathering around the glittering, broken glass on top of the wall of our small fortress in a strange land.

'Well,' Mark said, voicing my exact thoughts and fears. 'We're on our own now, Reverend!'

CHAPTER SIX

We slept, eventually, lulled by the unfamiliar noises that alarmed us for the first couple of restive hours. Being under the big white mosquito net was only temporarily claustrophobic, taking on as it did all the cosy properties of a tent, with the added luxury of being able to see through it. Remembering the anti-malaria tablets we had been taking since last week, it was comforting to know we were also protected against the effects of being bitten by the whirring little insects which we soon discovered did indeed come out at night.

We woke, simultaneously, realising that someone was rattling the gate downstairs. Our travelling alarm clock said 6.30 am, and Wilomenah had arrived to start her day's work. While Mark went to let her in, I looked around me, listening to the sound of a cockerel crowing below, and thought, 'I'm in Africa!' Looking at my battered Sunday-school Bible, in pride of place on the wicker dresser, I still wondered if it were all a dream. In our prayers the night before, we had thanked God heartily for bringing us here safely to what seemed like comparative comfort. As Wilomenah went into the spartan kitchen, I was reminded of my misgivings of the previous night.

'I prepare eggs now for breakfast,' she stated, beaming over the tray a few minutes later. Deftly, she put covered plates in front of us, and then went back for the thermos flask. 'Then I wash your clothes.'

'I haven't seen a washing machine,' I whispered to Mark as we finished giving thanks for the fried eggs and margarine sandwiches. The sound of running water came from the bathroom where Wilomenah was already busy, pounding with strong hands and bare feet the clothes in which we had travelled. I already knew from my attempt at bathing that the water was cold. We had been really grateful for our electric kettle, heating water to wash our hair and take a 'bucket' shower.

With the help of blue washing powder and a big plastic tub, our cook/housekeeper soon had everything spotless and pegged out on the balcony to dry.

'We all work so,' she smiled, sounding surprised when I expressed my admiration of her skills. Taking me to the window, she pointed into the yard next door where a girl of about twelve was doing the family laundry by hand, also in a plastic bucket. 'Even my maid at home. She will wash all my children's clothes so!'

Mark and I exchanged a look of surprise. 'You have a maid too? So, while you're cooking for us . . . ?'

'She cooks and cleans for me. Yes. Here in Kenya it is a must.' Taking a break from her work, Wilomenah explained that her maid was a member of her own tribe whom she had brought to Nairobi from the rural area. 'Mostly I work at the hospital,' she said. 'And she looks after the house. She is like my sister.'

'So do you feel better now?' Mark asked me later, as Wilomenah went to make the bed. 'Knowing our cook has got a cook?'

I smiled. Strangely enough, I did. Hearing our helper singing a hymn as she worked, I realised how lucky we were going to be, not only to have her practical services but to learn at first hand what life for her and her family was really like.

Suddenly a screech of brakes came from outside, followed by the tooting of a horn. 'Julius is here,' Wilomenah announced. 'His car is working again today, praise God!' As the tall young man stepped out of the battered vehicle, she went onto the balcony to call him up the stairs. 'I tell him what food he must bring from the hospital.'

After greeting us, Julius followed Wilomenah deferentially into the kitchen where she reeled off what seemed like an unending list of provisions. Although Ancrum had assured us our grocery shopping, like all our other domestic arrangements, would be done for us, it seemed strange not to be in control of what went into our own pantry.

'Shall we take care of the shopping, Julius?' I asked as we climbed into the car. 'I'm sure you've got other things to do around the hospital!'

Our driver looked at me in surprise. 'I will give the list to the caterer at the hospital, and she will send someone to the market,' he explained. 'It would not be easy for you to buy these things here for yourselves.'

As he put the car into gear and we jolted forward onto the road, I forgot everything in the renewed nightmare of eastern Nairobi street conditions. It was with a lot of relief, and even more thankful prayers that I found myself face to face with the single-storey building labelled 'Metropolitan Hospital'.

The hospital was set incongruously in the middle of Jericho Market, a smaller, more condensed version of Jogoo Road, with piles of avocado, pawpaw, mango and passion fruit stacked high on ramshackle stalls. Biodegradable garbage lay in piles, smoking and rotting in the growing heat of the day, yards from where milk was being sold, straight from a churn. On a nearby bench, a man sold corn, browned over a charcoal fire, while in the distance, a display of cheap necklaces and metal ear-rings flashed and dazzled in the sunlight.

Tooting his way cheerfully through the crowds, Julius took us over a ramp and through the hospital entrance. We saw a clean white exterior, with nurses in dark blue at the outpatients' desk. Over the top was a logo— Jesus on the cross, with wings like those of an angel. I felt a strange glow of warm recognition as I looked at it.

We left the car and were led around the side of the building to a set of primitive wooden steps which led, to my surprise, into what looked like the roof area of the hospital.

'This is the office,' Julius explained. We passed over a platform and through a door and were immediately enclosed by an unfinished structure, comprising concrete blocks, huge rafters and a corrugated metal roof. The space was full of occupied desks holding phones, computers and typewriters, all attached haphazardly to what looked like loose electricity wires. There were no windows, and rotary fans whipped round and round, trying unsuccessfully to stir the still and heavy air. At the reception desk, Rose looked up and saw us and quickly made a call on the inside phone. A moment later, Dr Gakombe came from the furthest end of the roof space, his hand extended in welcome.

'First the guided tour,' he said. 'As you will

see, in some things the hospital is doing well, in others we still need a lot of work, support and prayer.'

He explained that in Kenya there was no subsidised health care. 'People still die from malaria, typhoid, TB and, of course, Aids,' he said. 'It is very much a case of those who can pay will live and the others will die. We do have outreach programmes to the slums, and of course there is the Samaritan fund, run by Mr Evans and our Mr Moses Tibi. But people need spiritual support too, and that is why we are hoping you can help us set up the chaplaincy.'

Along with Matron, a well-spoken, intelligent woman in her thirties, we followed the doctor around the wards, seeing basic equipment, iron beds, huddled figures, some wearing anoraks in spite of the heat of the day.

'We are always short of basic commodities, bedding, crockery, kettles, irons,' Dr Gakombe explained, as he took us into the brightly decorated children's ward. 'Though sometimes appliances aren't much good because of the power cuts.'

He explained that because of the ever-growing demands of new consumers, the electricity supply in and around the city was very temperamental. 'We have our own generator now,' he went on. 'But you can imagine the trauma when the power goes off for several hours, particularly when you have babies in incubators.'

The outpatients' clinic was very full, reminding me of such hospital departments in England.

'Our fees are quite reasonable compared to the big government places,' Dr Gakombe told me. 'We tend to get patients who walk long distances for treatment.'

As we passed through on our way to the laboratory, I caught a glimpse of small, dark-skinned babies, held protectively in their mothers' arms, of two men with horrific burns, livid pink holes in the flesh of their arms and hands, of, incongruously, a thin, lethargic English woman, talking in a hoarse whisper to the restless, equally washed-out teenaged girl at her side on the bench.

'We even get the odd *muzunga* who's travelled to the rural area and been poisoned by the water!' the doctor grinned, following the direction of my eyes. 'Though I must admit, they are very few and far between.'

CHAPTER SEVEN

'I must ring Sarah!' At the back of my mind, the niggle went on. Dr Gakombe had tried to help, sitting patiently opposite us at his desk, dialling the international calls number over and over again.

'Sorry,' he said eventually. 'The lines are completely blocked. Generally, it is better to try in the evening, though in this case it's probably quicker if we ask Rose to fax Mr Evans. He will then send a message to your daughter.'

It seemed a bit complicated, but we had no choice. So we left the hospital, having to trust the family would eventually hear news of us.

St Stephen's, Church of the Province of Kenya, stood on the corner of Jogoo Road next to a dusty petrol station. Its compound was flanked by hawkers, their now familiar wares spread out on the ground feet away from the busy highway. The church itself was built of grey stone blocks and had a huge square tower, its windows open, overlooking the insalubrious side of the sprawling city. Leaving Julius to wait for us, we walked through the south doors and into a vastness which took our breath away.

'Why it's as big as an English cathedral!' I whispered wonderingly, as we walked echoing down the aisle towards the high altar, with its plain wooden cross. 'You could get two of St Mark's in here!'

It was the first time I had ever thought of my church at home as being anything but enormous, and I blinked as I tried to make the mental adjustment. Before Mark could reply, the vestry door opened and a smiling African clergyman came out.

'*Jambo*, my friends!' he said, shaking our hands warmly. 'I am Nick Ajoga, the curate. Welcome! We have been expecting you.'

We were led into the vestry where a group of six men sat around a table. Each rose in turn to greet us with a handshake and a word of introduction. The curate then invited us to draw up spare chairs and join them for worship.

Accustomed as I was to traditional Morning Prayer, I was both surprised and delighted by the spontaneity of the worship. The men, who comprised all the staff of the church from cleaners to lay readers, clapped and sang Swahili choruses, gave impromptu testimonies, and prayed aloud. Each had his own obviously much-read Bible.

After the worship, one of the younger men disappeared for a long time, reappearing eventually with a big tin teapot and a tray full of glass mugs. 'You take *chai*?' he said, going back for another tray of bread and margarine. 'First, we pray.'

Thanks were given, and then, as we tucked into the simple yet appetising food, the Reverend Nick began to tell us the history of the church. 'It was built before Independence, in the 1950s,' he said, nodding proudly. 'As you can see, it is a very, very old church!'

As Mark and I exchanged smiles, remembering my 146-year-old church back home, Nick went on to describe the many activities that took place at St Stephen's.

'We have three Sunday services, the first, at 7 am, in Swahili. That is not very well attended, only about 250 people. At 9 am, there is the English service, where we have 1,200 people, then at 11 comes another Swahili service, which is attended by 1,000.'

'So that's about 2,500 people every single Sunday?' I tried to take it in. 'I suppose that includes the Sunday school?'

'Oh no, my sister!' The curate reached over to slap hands with me, his brown eyes laughing at my astonishment. 'Sunday school is in the hall. For that we have about 600 children at each service.'

Showing us around a few minutes later, he described his typical week in ministry. 'We have problems as clergy do in England,' he said, 'with having too much to do and not enough hours in the day. But the pastoral work here is very different.'

He described the great poverty in certain areas of Nairobi, particularly the slums, and the tribalism which still existed in the country as a whole, making true Christian unity still an impossibility.

'It is still very true that if a man in authority is a Kikuyu then he will be inclined to help only Kikuyus, or if a Luo, only Luos,' he explained. 'There is much corruption here, and the church, or certain members of it, do from time to time speak out. But it can be dangerous, and sometimes it is safer to look the other way when you see people giving and accepting bribes.'

I remembered the notice at the airport, and began to understand something of what it meant. 'You mean the people who can afford to pay what we call back-handers can always get what they want, no matter who else has to suffer!'

'That's right,' Reverend Nick nodded. 'When you see the city you will understand that it is two very different worlds, with the poor very poor, and the rich living in what most of us would describe as heaven. And in the rural area, where my ancestral home is, things are even more disparate.'

He went on to explain that all Africans have two homes: the place where they have to be in order to earn a living, and the place where they originated, where their ancestors, dead and alive, still stayed.

'Perhaps you will have an opportunity to visit western Kenya while you are here, my brother and sister,' he said. 'In the meantime, when would you both like to come and preach to us?'

'Preach to over a thousand?' I later said to Mark, as Julius drove us back to Doonholm for lunch. 'That's something we definitely weren't trained for at theological college!'

Mark grinned. 'Just remember, the Lord has brought us here,' he said. 'Whatever he wants us to do, he won't expect us to do it in our own strength. Apart from that, we've got tonight's outreach service to break us in gently!'

Before we left St Stephen's, Nick had told us about the weekly services which were held on the local housing estates. 'Tonight I am going to Mbotela,' he'd said. 'I should like you both to join me and get to know the elders there.'

At 6 pm prompt we were back at the church to meet him, to be told his car had broken down and our transport would be needed. 'It is not far,' he said, jumping in beside Julius, 'but there are no street lights so I hope you have brought torches.'

As the car jerked forward in the gathering gloom, I stared through the darkened windows. At 7 pm it would be pitch dark, one of the things we were having to get used to since coming to live on the Equator. Turning off the Jogoo Road, we entered an area of tin shacks, a kind of shanty town which Nick explained was a 1950s council estate for workers. Traders were still operating from shacks lit by oil lamps, their glow casting yellow shadows on livid, purple joints of meat hanging behind dingy glass and covered in flies.

There were people everywhere, barefoot, busy, carrying bundles and water containers on their heads, burdened down by the very tangible weight of their daily lives. By the side of the narrow dirt-track roads were the now familiar piles of garbage, devoured by wandering livestock. But for the first time, perhaps because of the looming darkness, I noticed that there were also beautiful flowers growing alongside the filth, their colours amazingly bright and clean.

The place where Nick told us to stop was a wooden building in a pool of yellow electric light. We stumbled inside, fighting off the hungry mosquitoes, and were at once engulfed by welcoming people of all ages and both sexes.

'This is a nursery school in the day time,' Nick explained proudly. 'It is run by Agnes here, one of the elders.'

Agnes, a woman in her twenties, came forward to show us the nursery equipment. The walls had crude numbers painted on them, and there were a few exercise books and crayons and a lump of plasticine with which she demonstrated how the children learned to spell out the letters of their names. Looking around, I thought how different it all was to the nursery where Sarah worked, which had every commodity imaginable. The mosquitoes flew around as the door was opened again and again, letting in more and more people. They came to greet us and then went to sit on the rows of benches, bowing their heads in prayer.

When the place was full, Nick held up his hands. 'My brother here,' he said, clapping a

Bible-wielding elder on the back, 'is to lead our worship this evening. But first, we will all introduce ourselves. My name is Reverend Nick Ajoga, and I love the Lord Jesus.'

Then, one by one, they began to stand, from children to old ladies, giving their names and testimonies about what the Lord had done for them. Only one person, a middle-aged woman said, 'I'm not saved!' and she was greeted by warm laughter and affectionate nudging. 'Yet!' her nearest neighbours added meaningfully. There were choruses and dancing. Bible reading was led by the elder in charge, followed by all in their own Bibles.

Then, finally, it was our turn to speak. Nick had told them excitedly that we were visitors from England, and a very rare phenomenon— a husband and wife who were both pastors in different churches!

'My name is Mark,' my husband began, smiling, as the cheers and claps rose in the balmy air. 'And the Lord Jesus is my personal Saviour!'

Before I rose to speak, my heart swelling with the joy of the moment, I had the strangest sensation. The words that were being used, the enthusiasm, even the old-fashioned, rather tatty setting was taking me straight back—to my old Black Country Sunday school in the year 1954.

CHAPTER EIGHT

The next two weeks sped by, brimming with impressions, knocking us sideways time and again with tidal waves of culture shock. Used to instant communication, it continued to be painfully frustrating not to be able to pick up the telephone and talk to family and friends. I wrote long letters to everyone, trying not to sound wistful, trying to content myself with seeing the letters disappear into the 'out' tray at the hospital, to be delivered to the post office in Nairobi when someone happened to think about it.

Never again, I vowed, would I take our English postal system for granted. For I was learning the hard way what it meant to be a person 'care of' a post-office box number. Neither could we rely any more on electricity—it went off every day for several hours. It was the same with the water. By 10 am most mornings it would be impossible to flush the toilet or turn on the tap and so Wilomenah collected water, storing it wisely in all the buckets and jugs she could find.

These were problems that we had in common with all but the very rich inhabitants of Nairobi. We began to travel through the meanest parts of that city almost daily as we tried to forge links with local clergy, and each time we were shaken by what we saw.

A vast open vegetable market, stinking in the baking sun, set in an island of rotting vegetation, on which people sat and traded and tried to make a living. Dilapidated buildings with tattered hoardings and no windows. People standing in roadside puddles of stagnant water, washing their feet and legs as if they were in a hot bath. Lepers extending stumps, their blind eyes without a single vestige of hope. Children begging, following the car, hands outstretched, plastic glue bottles dangling from their nostrils. Every street corner a would-be bargaining place for fruit, for newspapers and magazines, for lame and crippled beggars. Pictures for sale everywhere of President Daniel arap Moi, and Jesus at the Last Supper.

How different it all was to 'Westlands' where tourists stayed in western-style hotels and went to game parks, shopping malls and restaurants. It was no surprise at all to find the map of Nairobi actually ended before it reached the parts our eyes and noses were growing to know so well. Our western sensibilities struggled with the injustice of it all. How could the Kenyans accept these living conditions in this century? Given that they paid their rates and taxes, why didn't they rise up and protest against the state of the infrastructure? Why did they just accept the poverty and deprivation that seemed to be the lot of so many of them?

Wilomenah tried to explain. 'We know that God is going to work a miracle,' she said, smiling as she carried in a pile of snowy washing from the balcony. 'Even for my five children. He will make sure that they have enough to eat and they will grow strong and well. It will all become right in his time.'

'I wonder if God's time is African time?' I mused, as Mark and I sat in St Stephen's the next Saturday, waiting for a bride who was two and a half hours late.

The Reverend Nick, who had invited us to help with the readings, grinned thoughtfully. 'We have started charging a deposit,' he said, 'of 3,000 Kenyan shillings. If the wedding party arrives on time, after collecting the bride from her family, they get it back. At the moment, 60 per cent lose the deposit. You see, this African time you speak of is very interesting, my sister.'

We sat watching the noon-day heat rise in the enormous building, its wilting altar flowers caught in the glow of the sun.

'It goes like this. I say I'll come and see you, not at 9 am but "early morning". That can be from 6 am to 10 am. Or "mid morning". That can be any time—'

'Until noon?' I suggested.

'Ah no, my sister!' he grinned expansively. 'That is too specific. Any time until the middle of the day, then we come to early afternoon,

41

late afternoon, early evening, late evening.'

'Sounds good to me,' Mark murmured, and I knew he was thinking of the slavery of diaries and time schedules that bound our parish ministry in the West.

'We have a saying here, my brother,' our new philosopher friend said. 'The white man has the watches, but the African has the time!'

Much of *our* weekday time was spent at the hospital where, sweltering under the tin roof of the office, we tried, with Rose's help, to contact anyone who might be interested in seeing us about the chaplaincy scheme.

'Ancrum's list of names is comprehensive, to say the least,' Mark commented as we looked at the half dozen pages of closely written names and addresses. 'There must be forty people here!'

They ranged from curates to cabinet ministers, reflecting our patron's indefatigable enthusiasm for his project. Because of the unreliability of the telephone or Julius' car being broken down or unavailable, we learnt to sit for hours. Passing the time with the staff whose faces and names were slowly becoming familiar. Watching patients as they made their way through the reception and into the waiting room. We saw every complaint from typhoid to malaria. We saw people on the brink of death, and women about to give birth. As we grew accustomed to the routine of the hospital, we became increasingly aware of the scourge of

Aids.

'It is our biggest problem,' Dr Gakombe told us solemnly. 'So many young people and nothing we can do. There are clinics and schemes which try to educate people, but in our first year we have had to close two wards because of this disease.'

One of the heartening things about the hospital was its overt Christian emphasis, as demonstrated by both the growing Samaritan fund and the monthly prayer breakfasts, the latter instigated by Ancrum when he came for the Metropolitan's official opening. Mark and I turned up rather nervously for the first of these prayer breakfasts at 7.30 am on our second Saturday in Kenya, a bright, clear day in April. We had been told the prayers began at 7.30 am but of course we were in African time now, and only the cleaner was around. There was no evidence whatsoever that anyone, least of all a group of local clergy, was expected, and so we relaxed on the wooden balcony, talking and waiting. By 8.15 the office roof space was full of people all eager to sing and pray and share in the early morning fellowship.

Mark and I, as visitors, had been invited to lead this month's worship and we were able to share something of the 'God-incidences' which had brought us to Africa. 'We still don't know exactly why we're here,' I finished a bit self-consciously as I held up my battered Bible.

'But getting a chaplaincy started at the hospital is certainly part of it.'

Moses Tibi, the director of the Samaritan fund, spoke for a long time about his vision for a chapel building as well as a chaplaincy rota at the Metropolitan. 'Funds are being raised in England, at Lower Sapey,' he said, 'but in the meantime we must encourage people to pray that the right leaders will come forward to run it.'

Remembering our trips around Nairobi, the phone calls which hadn't been very fruitful, we knew from our own experience that most ministers are very busy, and with the size of congregations, that had to be specially true in Kenya. However kindly disposed they might be to the idea of voluntary chaplaincy at a new hospital, they might not, physically, be able to help, even on a part-time basis.

'We'll get them,' Mark said determinedly as he took out Ancrum's list again. 'We've already got appointments with a few more pastors next week. And don't forget, we're preaching at St Stephen's on Sunday. Then everyone'll know we're here.'

I swallowed as I thought of Reverend Nick's description of the enormous church on a typical Sunday morning, with over 2,000 rapt African faces. 'That's what I'm afraid of!' I said weakly.

CHAPTER NINE

'Praise the Lord!' I said quickly into the microphone. The response from the oceans of black faces on all sides was instantaneous. 'Amen!' they all called, waving their left hands in greeting. Encouraged, I waved my own rather shaky left hand. 'Praise the Lord again!' I declared.

It was certainly what we were in St Stephen's for! As I got under way with my sermon, a favourite topic about St Paul on the road to Damascus, I noticed the congregation was perfectly still, intent on what I was saying. People of all ages had brought Bibles, and they turned to them as I read from the Book of Acts. I couldn't help but compare their involvement with the generally more lukewarm response from English Anglican congregations. Here, the sermon was simply accepted as a word from the Lord, the preacher the mouthpiece or instrument. All was to God's glory, and that was especially true of the singing that followed.

There was singing from the youth group, a vivacious crowd of teenagers who bounced into the chancel to sway and clap their way through Swahili choruses. There was singing from the Sunday school, many hundreds of them who crowded into the same space, and, to the accompaniment of a drum, gave us their interpretation of praise. Then there was the choir itself, resplendent in red robes with white mantles. Expertly led by the choirmaster, they demonstrated just how long they practised the complicated Swahili melodies. Again they were accompanied by drumbeat, and again they swayed and clapped. The whole thing was interspersed by imitation bird songs and cries of almost inarticulate joy, like yodelling from the very heart.

'It's totally amazing!' I whispered to Mark as he stepped out to get a photograph. 'And it's been going on for hours!'

It was true that the people of St Stephen's had been praising the Lord since 7 am. It was now 11.30 am and there was much, much more to come. When it came to Holy Communion, we stared, thrilled and astonished, to see six bottles of communion wine and many containers of wafers brought to the altar. Half a dozen chalices stood ready, waiting to be filled. The prayer of consecration was said by the presiding archdeacon, and then, in a daze, we were ushered forward to assist with the distribution.

'How on earth are we going to get through them all?' Mark whispered. Our only similar experience was at cathedrals in England, where certain points were designated for distribution. But here everyone was coming to the front!

'You do this section, sister.' Nick handed me a paten full of wafers and pointed me towards a stretch of the altar rail.

'The body of Christ,' I began the familiar chant, the light wafers dropping from my fingers into the pink-palmed, unfamiliar hands. Hands that appeared time and time again until the paten was empty. And still more people to come!

The service finally ended with a large procession all down the centre aisle and out through the main doors. Once outside, we stood in a circle, choir, acolytes, robed lay readers and clergy, and carried on singing. The hymn was 'We're marching to Zion', and it swelled from the thousand Christians still singing their hearts out in the church behind us.

'My brother.' The archdeacon, beaming, but very much in charge, held out his hand in invitation to Mark. 'Would you dismiss us please?'

Mark gave the dismissal and the group disbanded. But the praising still went on, people shaking hands, greeting us and one another, endlessly saying, *'Bwana Asifiwe!* Praise the Lord!' as they came out into the sunshine.

Life itself is full of praise here, I realised as Julius drove through the crush and picked us up to go home. In the afternoon, when we switched on the rather flickering television set, it was to see a Christian programme with prayers and a sermon. The day before, we had heard on the radio, also at peak time, a man expounding on the Book of Job. To us, coming from a society where *Songs of Praise* was thought of as keeping old ladies happy at Sunday tea-time, it was more than an eye-opener—it was a revelation!

'In Kenya,' I wrote to my colleague Charles next day, 'it's thought quite normal to talk about Jesus!'

CHAPTER TEN

On the corner of Jogoo Road, directly opposite St Stephen's, we discovered an English oasis. The Church Army Training College had been in existence there since before Independence, and slowly but surely had put down roots. To us, alien *wuzungu* in a strange land, those roots bore comforting and familiar fruit. Green lawns and flushing toilets, a students' dining hall, books which could be borrowed from the Church Army library, even a dog which wagged its tail instead of scurrying, cur like, among the garbage heaps.

The director was an Englishman whose wry sense of humour brightened many an anxious day. 'You know where to come if you get really desperate,' he grinned, after showing us the crowded dental clinic, lecture halls and primary school which stood on the enclosed compound. 'You can even come out to my place for a hot bath when you feel you can't stand the bucket any longer!'

'I'll remember that, Stanley,' I promised. After finally hearing from Sarah, Edmund and friends back home, I felt less disturbed, though it was still difficult not to be in control of our communications.

'We're keeping our lines open to God, anyway,' Mark reminded me as we swatted mosquitoes in the living room and prepared to say our regular evening prayers. Aware of our vulnerability, our reliance on strangers whose culture was so different, we knew we had to trust ourselves to him, knowing he had brought us here for his own purpose, and that one day we would find out what that purpose was.

There was so much poverty and need. Each morning, we watched from behind our barred windows as a woman came like a beast of burden to the building site opposite, carrying a bowl on her head and a bundle in the bowl. At her side was her small, barefoot son, dragging an empty milk carton on a bit of string as a toy car. Earlier, the blanket-clad Masai night-watchman had left his sentry box opposite and, putting down his bow and steel-tipped arrow, had coaxed the woman's fire into life. Now she busied herself, unwrapping her cloth-wrapped bundles, sending the boy for water, tying her faded skirt around herself as she prepared to start her cooking.

'You have seen the workmen come,' Wilomenah reminded us matter of factly. 'This woman cooks breakfast and lunch for them for a few shillings. It is the only way for her to live.'

The huddled figures crouching on the bare earth were a familiar sight and we watched wonderingly as the woman distributed plastic bowls full of the thin maize porridge. Later, the small boy would wobble over from the fire, carrying a tin teapot almost as big as himself.

Even when the long rains started, neither the woman nor her customers were deterred, some coming from nearby houses to eat 'al fresco'. One regular client even came in a car, parking it in the mud and treading seemingly without a care for his shining shoes and smart grey business suit.

'Pray God she has a licence,' our invaluable informant went on thoughtfully, as the woman collected her payments. 'If she does not, they will chase her away from there.'

'They?' I frowned. It wasn't the first time we had been uncomfortably aware of what we could only describe as the 'Big Brother' syndrome. It had something to do with the determined playing of the Kenyan national anthem so regularly on the radio. And the way each and every news bulletin, on TV and radio, began with the words, 'President Daniel arap Moi *today* . . . !'

It was all very different to our life in England which we were urged to talk about on our visits to clergy and our rather tenuous invitations to prayer groups and Mothers' Union meetings. Wherever we went we were greeted excitedly, almost rapturously, so that we often felt overwhelmed by the sometimes harrowing stories of the people we met. One middle-aged Kikuyu woman, Sheila, a stalwart member of St Stephen's Mothers' Union, gave a wonderful testimony of being healed from a back injury.

'I lay in the Kenyata Hospital, and I heard the Lord Jesus say to me, "Take up your bed and walk," just like he said to the paralysed man,' she recounted, as we sat around the steaming milky tea in the vestry. 'I got up and walked across the ward, and the nurses couldn't believe it. I tell you, my sister, it was a miracle!'

Sheila was so grateful for her miracle that she decided to try and help others in need. 'I work in an office in Nairobi,' she explained, 'and every day I see these children living in the streets.'

We all nodded, recalling the disturbing sights we too had seen. 'The Lord said I should help them, take them food and clothes and pray with them. I have begun, but they are so many and I am but one.'

She described how she spent her lunch breaks with the street children, listening to their stories and trying to befriend them. 'They do not trust adults. Many of them have been raped or sodomised, beaten by grown-ups all their lives. But I told them God loves them.'

'He does,' I agreed. But sadly I wondered, what evidence would the street children be able to find for such a statement?

The whole difference between African and European culture seemed to be summed up in Sheila's next words. 'I told them God *must* love them because although they eat from the garbage in the streets, they do not get sick, whereas the rich tourists in the best hotels are always getting bad stomachs. And though they have only ragged clothes to wear, they do not get colds, while those who have much to wear are always shivery and sneezing.'

Gradually, we were being drawn closer to people whose reliance on God put us to shame. Clergy with vast congregations and no means of transport, who could scarcely afford to support their families; hospital patients whose only hope when faced with massive hospital bills was to pray; those who were moved by the Holy Spirit to arrange impromptu *harambees* or collections for church or individual needs—a case of literally holding out a basket and asking people to show their love for God and for their neighbours by digging deep into almost empty pockets.

'*Bwana Asifiwe!*' all would declare, as another tiny miracle took place.

Isolated on our building site, getting accustomed to faulty services and no means of communication, we found ourselves building even more on the 'God-incidences' we had relied on to bring us here. And looking for miracles ourselves.

CHAPTER ELEVEN

'Are you going to St Stephen's?' The dark head poked through the window of the car that Sunday morning was undoubtedly the answer to a prayer. And a very frenzied one at that.

We had woken early to the novelty of getting our own breakfast, something we did after insisting that Wilomenah have her weekends free. I was due to preach at St Stephen's and had decided to take as my text the words 'trust and obey', giving the now familiar testimony of how the Lord had tirelessly called me to Kenya. The English service was scheduled to begin at 9 am, although we now knew from experience that the congregation would drift in long after that time.

By 8.30 am, the time we had asked to be collected, we were all ready, our robes and books placed carefully on the sofa within grabbing distance. All we needed was the welcome sight of Julius' car appearing through the dust to carry us on our way, and we went out onto the balcony to look for him.

For once, the unmade road was quiet, the Sunday atmosphere entirely different to the busy weekday one. The people who drifted past were obviously on their way to church, splashing through the mud in their best clothes, many of them with small children in tow. There was no sign of the car, and as the time went by, we became more and more anxious. St Stephen's was not within walking distance, we had no means of contacting anyone, and it was now 8.45 am!

'What can we do?' I asked worriedly. 'We can't just let everybody down when they're expecting me to preach!'

'Let's pray,' Mark suggested. So we went back inside, sat down opposite each other and asked God for his help. We were sure he would get us there somehow, but when the minutes continued to tick by and there was still no sign of Julius, we decided we had no alternative but to literally 'step out in faith'. It was 8.55 when we turned the corner by the shack selling charcoal and began to walk towards the dusty Outer-ring Road. Our white faces were, as always, a source of curiosity and interest, and those people who did not smile and greet us with a cheerful 'Jambo!' stopped dead and stared.

We were caught up in a flow of people which, although still not as dense as the weekday traffic, was still purposefully moving, making their way to the many churches in and around the city. Suddenly, a *matatu* jangled beside us, almost brushing my side as it veered towards the pavement. The tout, his eyes lighting up at the prospect of two white passengers in clerical collars, jumped off, urging us to get aboard. 'Where do you want to go, pastor? We give you a ride!'

As he held out his hand for the fare, I looked up at the swaying vehicle, packed already with passengers who seemed to be sitting on top of one another. It was as we hesitated, reluctant to see this as the answer to our prayer, that the car pulled up alongside the gaudy bus.

'I saw you at the fellowship meeting on Thursday,' the woman explained as we thankfully climbed inside. 'My name is Angela, and I love the Lord Jesus.'

'So do we!' I exclaimed, catching Mark's eye. We sped along, onto the Jogoo Road, all our worries about being late forgotten.

At 9.10 am, we were robed and in St Stephen's vestry, soon to follow the magnificent choir down the vast aisle which reverberated with the massed African voices.

'How shall we get home?' I asked Mark, as I checked my sermon was still tucked into the dilapidated Bible. 'We didn't ask Angela if she was going back our way, and in any case, we've got the Swahili service after this.'

My husband smiled towards the simple cross that was the focal point of our service. '*Hakuna matata!*' he whispered. After our morning's experience I knew he was absolutely right. With God as our helper and guide, it was 'no problem' at all!

As we neared the end of our first month in Kenya, we realised that our efforts towards establishing a chaplaincy at the Metropolitan Hospital needed to be both intensified and co-ordinated. Following Ancrum's list of contacts, we had discovered several local clergy who were quite willing to attend monthly prayer breakfasts and to visit patients from their own congregations. Some, like Reverend Jeff Mambo of St Paul's, Buruburu, told horrific stories of neglect, bribery and simple shortage of medical equipment at the established government hospitals. All were enthusiastic about the Samaritan fund, and said they would encourage the better-off members of their congregations to become shareholders. Most invited us to preach at their churches, so that all our Sundays and most of our weekdays were soon booked up well in advance.

What we were really looking for though, as Dr Gakombe and the staff readily agreed, was a committed and experienced hospital chaplain willing to run the chaplaincy once we had returned to the UK. We prayed about this regularly, both at home and sitting on the shady bench at the side of the hospital, a bench we had affectionately dubbed 'the chaplain's office'. It stood near the patch of weed-covered ground where Dr Gakombe had told us the hospital chapel would one day stand.

'It'll soon be time to tell the clergy about the next prayer breakfast,' Mark said one day. The sun seemed to have disappeared, and Wilomenah had started shivering at what she called the 'coldiness' in the air. 'We can start at the Presbyterian church this afternoon!'

The Presbyterian church at Bhahati was a long, one-storey building in a compound where children played on dusty car tyres and people passed on foot on their way to and from work and to fetch water. As the plaque outside proudly told us, the church had been built as a monument. It was a martyrs' church, erected in honour of the Kikuyu Christians who had died at the hands of the Mau Mau.

Our appointment with the pastor was at 4 pm, and we were a few minutes early. 'The pastor is not back,' the smiling church secretary who greeted us explained. 'But he will not be long, if you would like to wait.'

We stood outside, happy to watch the passing traffic of pedestrians. The atmosphere was totally relaxed, our growing knowledge and acceptance of African time making us unworried about the pattern for the rest of the day. We yawned and talked and enjoyed the fading sunshine. We were soon joined by a youth worker, a young woman who told us, eyes shining with pride, that theirs was called a 'drive-in church'. 'So many people come here on Sundays that the church cannot hold them,' she explained. 'So the service is relayed by loud speakers outside, and people have the books and sing and pray in their cars!'

She pointed to a big, strange-looking building beyond the church compound. 'That is our new church,' she said. 'Would you like to look inside?'

Collecting the keys, she led us through a gate across some rough grassland and into the church building. Then, we both caught our breath. For though the building looked clumsy from the outside, inside it was truly magnificent in both scale and vision.

'It's like a Greek amphitheatre!' I exclaimed, looking across to the gallery where thousands of seats had been cut, literally, out of the stone. The acoustics were amazing, as was the visual impact, because all attention was drawn to the front, into the vast chancel area.

'Here is where our preacher will stand,' our guide said, as first Mark and then I tried out the spot. 'As you can see, everyone will be able to see and hear them.'

58

She led us round, showing off other features: the sound-proofed room where nursing mothers could go and feed their babies while still being part of the service; the offices and meeting rooms at the back.

'It will hold over 3,000 people,' she told us casually. 'And look, here is our cross.'

She pointed out a huge metal cross, lying along one of the aisles. 'This will be put over the altar, and another will go on the outside of the church.'

'And all this started with the drive-in church?' I asked, as we walked back into the compound.

'Oh yes,' the young woman smiled, 'but that is not unusual here. Many churches begin even more simply, in a tent.'

After she had left us, we resumed our leisurely wait for the pastor. In spite of the procession of people who still continued to file past, there was all around us an air of peace, as if God knew exactly what he was doing, and there was no need for us to worry about a thing. We had almost forgotten why we had called to see Pastor Jesse, the hospital ministry on another level of consciousness as we sat and dreamed. How great it would be to see a church like this one back in England, with enough people willing and eager to fill it. Enough new Christians growing closer to the Lord!

As we talked, a car suddenly drew into the

compound. 'This must be the pastor,' Mark said, getting to his feet. Instead of a clergyman, however, we saw a tall, athletic Kikuyu woman in a bright, floral dress. Getting out of the driving seat, she stepped into the sunlight. We had never set eyes on her before. But in the open, African manner we were getting used to, she strode out the distance between us.

'*Jambo!*' she began, holding out a broad, capable hand. 'My name is Jemima Ngatia. I love the Lord Jesus Christ, and for many years I have been serving him as a hospital chaplain. Who are you please?'

CHAPTER TWELVE

'We shouldn't really be surprised!' we kept on telling each other. But we were, and the surprise only added to our joy and to our confidence in the Lord. This was, after all, what he had brought us to Africa for, wasn't it?

Jemima explained that, like us, she had come to the Presbyterian church that afternoon simply to see the pastor. She didn't know of our existence, although she had heard of the Metropolitan Hospital. It had been in the back of her mind for some time to explore the possibility of ministering there.

'I was trained in chaplaincy and pastoral care in the United States of America,' she told us proudly, as she sat on the wall beside us. 'Since then, I have been training others here at the Presbyterian church.'

She explained that although she was employed at a big Nairobi hospital, she was finding her work there more and more difficult, and was on the point of resigning. 'There are so many patients, so many needs, and the staff are not always open to the gospel,' she said sadly. 'I just want to do what the Lord has called and trained me to do.'

We were still trying to get over the new and amazing 'God-incidence' of meeting her in this way. For we didn't need anyone to tell us that if the pastor hadn't been late for his afternoon appointments that day, none of this would have happened.

'I really feel we're getting somewhere now,' Mark said as we later consolidated our plans at home. 'Especially if Jemima is willing, as she says, to come to the next prayer breakfast and tell us her vision of hospital chaplaincy, and her willingness to act as voluntary co-ordinator.'

'We can even think of having a chapel building,' I heard myself say, and remembering what I'd heard that day, 'even a tent would do to start off with.'

'We can have a tent put up for the final breakfast before we go home,' Mark suggested

61

thoughtfully. 'I wonder if Ancrum would agree?'

'There's only one way to find out,' I replied. 'We'll have to send him a fax.'

The fax was sent from the hospital next day, and within a few hours we had the reply. 'Send costing for tent hire or purchase, chairs, etc. Funds are available from Lower Sapey.'

'I know they had a few fund-raising events for us there last year,' Dr Gakombe said, as we excitedly showed him the fax. 'Mr Evans told us about them when he came over to open the hospital last year. Now you are getting things to happen, the money will come.'

Dr Gakombe had been delighted to hear of our encounter with Jemima Ngatia, and had arranged to meet her the following week to formally discuss her professional involvement with the hospital.

The May prayer breakfast was encouraging in that apart from staff and hospital directors, it was attended by several of the local clergy we had visited, including one from St Teresa's, in the slums. He told the harrowing story of a young man, badly savaged by dogs, who had been recently taken by his church members to a public hospital.

'First, the gate-keeper wanted a bribe, then the ward attendant. But the boy had no money. He waited from eight in the evening until three the next morning without receiving any medical attention. Finally, my wife, who was one of those who had accompanied him, telephoned me and asked, "What shall we do?" I told them to bring him here, to the Metropolitan, and he was treated at once.'

Dr Gakombe nodded. 'This is the beauty of the Samaritan fund. Even in these early days of implementation, it can really help in an emergency like that.'

We began by singing choruses and had a time of prayer led by Moses Tibi, the Samaritan fund director. His rich, deep voice carried us in the still, morning air, right to the heart of God as he sang a Swahili bidding. Then Jemima outlined her plans for the hospital chaplaincy. 'I have spoken with your director, and also your English visiting pastors,' she said, 'and they agree that at first we should visit the hospital twice weekly. We should get to know the patients, staff and visitors, and bring them all before the Lord in prayer.'

She was, she repeated, prepared to work on a voluntary basis, and she knew her students would too. In fact one of her students, a middle-aged lay reader from St Paul's, had come along that morning.

'My name is Priscilla,' she said, extending her hand to all in turn. 'The Lord Jesus is my personal Saviour, and I am happy to serve him!'

We spent a long time in discussion, agreeing that part of the chaplaincy work should be support for the staff.

'Reverend Carol?' asked one young nursing sister later, as we all enjoyed a breakfast of pawpaw, cold sausages and the obligatory margarine sandwiches. 'Would you please pray for my family? I have written our needs here.'

I nodded as I took the piece of paper. 'I'll be happy to, Cynthia,' I said.

Looking at the positive group, and feeling the warm presence of God around us, I knew that at least one aim of our mission here had been accomplished. We were already making a difference.

In smaller ways, it was also a privilege to be able to improve daily life for the people closest to us, without whose practical help we would have found it hard to survive. As I had hoped, Wilomenah became a special friend, someone who, by spending several hours a day in close contact with us, taught us what life for the average African worker was really like.

'My Christina was so happy with the socks you sent her!' she told me as she busied herself in the kitchen one morning. 'She had no socks to wear for school, and now she has this pair from England. I tell you, she washes them every day, and when she sleeps, she puts them on her pillow, like so!'

She placed her folded hands against her cheek, smiling her affection and gratitude. Through Stanley and the few other expatriates we had met, we had become aware of the great needs here for simple commodities that we took for granted in England. Biros and toothbrushes, toiletries and any kind of luxury goods were all rare and precious, and tights were as prized as nylon stockings had been in war-time Britain.

With Julius, too, we shared a special bond, mainly but not wholly because he was totally responsible for our transportation and safe arrival at our many meetings and church services. As Dr Gakombe's younger brother— a relationship we hadn't fully realised at first— he was privileged in being found driving work at the hospital. But the amount of work he did, and under stressful conditions, was phenomenal—his old car acting not only as a taxi for the staff, but as an ambulance for patients.

'I hit a pot-hole and the suspension was broken!' he would explain when arriving late, or explaining a prolonged absence from Doonholm. 'I must stay with the car in the garage while she is being fixed.'

We must have looked puzzled, for he explained quickly that if you did not stand and watch your car being mended, some mechanics were not above taking another, non-faulty part out of the engine and selling it to the next customer who came along.

CHAPTER THIRTEEN

Dr Yenko, whose flat we were renting, had been off sick with meningitis for several months, and was staying with his parents near the hospital. He returned to his duties in May, a quiet, delicate-looking young man who obviously needed to build up his strength before returning to Doonholm and life on his own.

'I am pleased that you are taking care of the flat for me,' he said. 'Let me know if you have any problems.'

The only major problem we encountered was when, for no apparent reason, our electricity supply was disconnected. It was off for a week, despite the bill being paid. Daily telephone calls from the hospital to the Kenya Power and Light Company resulted in daily promises that 'the reconnection team was on its way'. So we would go home and wait, and the sudden darkness of equatorial night would fall again. And still nothing happened.

Africans we spoke to in the churches and fellowship groups expressed no surprise. Some of them were disconnected regularly. Stanley at the Church Army put our fury and helpless frustration into a nutshell: 'It's happened to us so often now we call them "Kenya Powers of Darkness"! Come and see how the other half lives for a change. You can stay the night and tell us about the good things that are happening.'

It was a delight to be taken in Stanley's well-sprung car into the green part of Nairobi where he and his family lived. Their home was cool and comfortable without being opulent, and we found we could laugh at our passing hardships at Doonholm as we enjoyed a meal together. It was also a wonderful luxury to be able to take not one bath but two—one before bed, and the other before setting off back to Jogoo Road the next day.

I told myself I could even cope with the darkness after such an enjoyable break, especially as it also resulted in Stanley showing interest in the Metropolitan.

'Our students do some hospital chaplaincy in the course of their training,' he explained over the mangoes we had for breakfast. 'I'm sure we could work out some visits for them, particularly now you've found a co-ordinator.'

In every direction we turned, God seemed to be leading us to all the right people, and we had no doubt at all that Jemima and the hospital chapel-in-a-tent was the main reason he had brought us here. We began to visit the wards regularly, on Tuesday and Thursday as planned, meeting Jemima, Priscilla and other Christians in the car park, and making our way around the wards. Before we entered, Jemima would go to the reception desk and make inquiries about the patients, and was shown a list of names and conditions. If anyone was in special need, the nurse on duty would make a point of telling us. Those patients who had been diagnosed as having Aids or who were HIV positive were identified on the list. Jemima's specialist training in counselling was then invaluable.

'I will speak to her in her mother tongue,' she would say, approaching a patient with hand outstretched. 'Maybe she will want to talk.'

The hospital was the one place where we found language a barrier. Some of the older patients spoke no English and some had no Swahili. Unless we had an interpreter with us, we would sometimes feel useless and ill at ease.

'The Lord must be really enjoying the joke, sending me here to do this!' I said on more than one occasion as Mark and I set out for the hospital. We both knew that hospital visiting was the least favourite of all my ministerial duties back home. However, I did enjoy going round the maternity ward with Jemima, and many times would be asked to bless new-born babies and their mothers.

'Have you chosen the baby's name yet?' I asked the first time I held a tiny, dark-skinned infant. But I soon learnt that names were already chosen. Traditionally, a first-born son was called after his paternal grandfather, a first-born daughter for her paternal grandmother. Having four children ensured that each set of in-laws was satisfied. In some cases, heartbreakingly, babies would be born under the shadow of Aids, their mothers diagnosed as HIV positive. There was no way of knowing if these tiny scraps of humanity had inherited the disease, but we grew to recognise and to dread the look of apprehension and guilt in the faces of their sometimes pitifully young mothers.

'We need a real spiritual centre, not just a tent,' Kaenje Gakombe said when, our lights reconnected, we invited him and his wife for a celebration supper. 'Particularly if we are going to have these groups from the Church Army that you mention. I think we should fax Mr Evans again—ask if we cannot start with a wooden building . . .'

'A wooden building!' Mark, Moses Tibi and I stood among the weeds behind the chaplain's office bench. 'Dr Gakombe's right, because Jemima is already talking about having regular services, and a fellowship for the nurses. It would be good to have a permanent structure if all that's going on.'

'Let's pray.' Moses spread his hands and we drew closer together, the busy world of the nearby hospital and the noisy bustle of Jericho market seeming to fade away as we again drew closer to the source of our energy and inspiration.

'Make this a holy place, Lord. A place where people come to find healing and inner peace. A place of safety and of restoration for many souls.'

During the next few weeks, we saw, to our amazement, a new dimension to African time. It was *harambee* in action. Once the money arrived with a long fax of instructions from Ancrum, so did the timbers. And with the timbers came the workers—all ages and sizes, with all degrees of skill and experience. They swarmed across the weeds and began working: levelling the ground, laying cement, sawing, hammering, building wooden walls and then wooden ladders to reach the tops of them. Before our very eyes the building took shape, so that the tourist in us ran for the camera, snapping the developments before they disappeared into the next stage.

'We can plan an official open day some time in early June,' Mark planned. 'Raise plenty of interest before we have to leave.'

We might have known that the interest was already there, and as we visited churches for our Sunday engagements, we found we were asked questions about the Metropolitan and its new chapel. People from outside the hospital arranged to meet us outside the half-completed building, sharing their problems as they took advantage of our unexpected availability as counsellors.

'Please pray for me that I will be successful

in my job application.'

'I have this rash, and I wondered if you have seen anything like it in England.'

'Sister Carol, my family is suffering because our uncle died, and we have no funds for the medical bills he left behind.'

The problems were so varied, and many seemed insoluble. We had few available funds, and only the promise that we would use whatever contacts and influence we had to send back assistance, advice or other support once we got home. But though we often felt inadequate, those who had made the effort to come and see us showed no signs of being cast down or disappointed by our limitations. They seemed happy that we had listened, giving freely of our time. It was, we were realising more and more, a precious commodity that was in short supply in our busy ministries back in England.

CHAPTER FOURTEEN

'I can't believe another week is nearly over!' I said to Mark and Wilomenah as we sat waiting for Julius' car. It was the middle of May, our time in Kenya half over. Already the weather was changing, the sunny days of our arrival giving way to periods of heavy, prolonged rain, particularly at night.

Our daily life had settled into a simple routine of sleep, study and prayer which we vowed to try and retain on our return to the UK. We had learnt the lesson of living one day at a time, without letting that day be overloaded with frenetic activity. Highlights of each day were encounters with fellow Christians whose love for the Lord shone out of them, and we visited theological colleges in and around Nairobi, encouraged by the enthusiasm and faith of those who would soon be taking the gospel to others.

Evidence of that life-changing gospel was everywhere. From the sight of children skipping in the street and singing songs about Jesus, to the heart-warming sound of thousands of Africans worshipping all night long in St Stephen's church.

'We meet once a fortnight for this prayer meeting,' the archdeacon told us simply, surprised at our astonishment. 'It starts on Friday evening at eight and continues until dawn on Saturday.'

Similarly, the Living Word African Gospel church celebrated the filling of their marquee, announcing a *harambee* in order to raise funds for a more permanent building.

'They will take down the tent and you will see the timbers soon,' Wilomenah promised, eyes shining. 'Just like at the hospital. God's house will be built!'

Watching the Metropolitan chapel gradually

taking shape, realising plans for the open day were well in hand, we felt both relieved and strangely disconcerted. What next?

'It would be good for you to visit a game park,' Moses suggested, 'though not in Julius' car! I will see if I can borrow a landrover.'

Through Moses and other friends, we were able to spend a little time at the tourist spots such as the Animal Orphanage, the game park, and Giraffe Manor, as well as visiting the Karen Blixen museum, the Nairobi museum, and Bomas of Kenya where we saw wonderful tribal dancing. Wilomenah also insisted on taking us to the Masai craft market on the outskirts of Nairobi where, for the first time, we saw *wuzungu* out in force.

'The tourists come here to buy gifts and the Masai charge them many times the value,' she said. 'You stay with me and say nothing!'

The market was on a slithering mountain of mud, where natives sat with their wares on display—ornaments, jewellery, African clothes.

Immediately we got out of the car, we were swamped with eager tradesmen.

'Mama? You want to buy a stone elephant? I give you a good price!'

'Hey *Bwana*, you come this way! I show you many fine things!'

'You hold your money tight!' Wilomenah instructed. As we stopped near a stall, she asked the price of *lesos* (African wrap-around

73

skirts) which I wanted to see.

'Eighty shillings,' said the warrior stallholder.

'How many you want to buy?' Wilomenah asked me surreptitiously. 'Six? If we take six he will give me a good price.'

I nodded as I tried to picture all our female friends at home wrapped in the resplendent cotton garments. After bargaining in Swahili, Wilomenah at first shook her head and, motioning me to follow, prepared to walk scornfully away.

'Wait! Mama!' The young stallholder sighed, his face resigned above his beaded necklet. 'All right. For six, you have them for seventy shillings!'

My hand moved with relief to my neck purse, but was stopped by Wilomenah's quick nudge. She stood back, fingering the *lesos*, pretending lack of interest, regarding the stallholder thoughtfully.

'I have only sixty shillings for each one. That is four hundred and twenty shillings.'

The stallholder narrowed his eyes, looking from one to the other of us warily. I thought he would say firmly that there was no deal, but he obviously knew he had met his match.

'All right, Mama,' he sighed. 'For the *muzunga*. But you are robbing me very much.' His flashing smile was a contradiction as I handed over the money via Wilomenah and received the bundled *lesos*. A moment later, he was busy bargaining with a muslim woman clad from head to toe in black robes.

'He will have bought the *lesos* for forty shillings or less at the Somalie market,' Wilomenah consoled me as we hurried back to the waiting car. 'These people, they are very crafty.'

On the way back in the car, we talked of other trips and other treasures which we needed to buy before Mark and I went home. A drum for Andy. Something artistic for Edmund. Malachite jewellery for Sarah and Liz.

'There is much to buy here,' Wilomenah explained, 'because the Masai make the things where they stay and then walk many kilometres, starting before it is light, carrying so much on their heads!'

It was good to be able to share some of our impressions of everyday Kenyan life with our friends at the churches, and we happily compared the Masai market to the rather staid English markets we were used to at home. We were also pleased when visitors came to the flat: Moses and Jane Tibi, with their two tiny children; the hospital caterer, Pauline and her husband; Wilomenah's family of graceful teenagers. We organised sodas and awaited our guests' arrivals with interest and enthusiasm, grateful for so many new and like-minded friends.

The visitors whose coming was to have the

most dramatic repercussions on our future in Africa, however, were the most unexpected ones. We were just getting ready for bed one night when a car pulled up in the mud outside, and someone banged on the iron gates. It was pitch dark and raining heavily. Through the gloom, I saw the night-watchman's lurking shadow as Mark went onto the balcony to see who was there.

'It's Nick and Alice,' he said in surprise. 'I wonder what they want at this time of night?'

A moment later, the curate of St Stephen's stood, dripping, in our living room. His wife Alice stood at his side, smiling hopefully

'We are going on leave, to my ancestral home in western Kenya,' he said. 'We will be consecrating a church there—St Mark's, Konjra. And the Lord has told us because of St Mark's, England, you people *must* come with us!'

CHAPTER FIFTEEN

The battered white estate car drew up with a scream of brakes, skidding in the mud outside the gate.

'He is here!' called Wilomenah excitedly from the balcony. 'The pastor has come to take you on your safari!'

Mark and I looked at each other a little

nervously over our packed bags and mosquito net. In spite of our excitement about visiting another part of Kenya, we couldn't help feeling a bit apprehensive. In making the arrangements for our three-day visit to his 'ancestral home', Nick hadn't once mentioned where we would sleep. Instinctively, our thoughts had gone to mud huts in the back of beyond. Our fears had not been helped by Dr Gakombe's advice that Konjra was a malarial area and we must take special care to guard against the mosquitoes.

'Bye, Wilomenah!' Our cook had fussed over us, making sure we not only had enough clean, pressed clothes, but that we took bottles of cooled, boiled water for the journey.

'It is many hours to western Kenya,' she said knowledgeably, 'and the car may be full of people.'

The words came back to me as I stared at the vehicle which, *matatu*-like, was packed from floor to roof with squashed bodies and assorted luggage. Strapped precariously to the roof rack were two huge wooden doors.

'These are the doors to St Mark's church,' Nick explained, as he shook hands all round. 'We take them with us, for the service.'

It was a warm day in spite of the season of long rains, and as we ducked and squeezed inside the vehicle, Mark taking the front passenger seat, I wondered how on earth we were going to survive a 'many-hour' journey.

'This is my daughter, Annika,' Nick introduced us to a slim, pretty teenager at my side. 'She is going to work. We will drop her in town. Alice has gone on ahead in the overnight bus, but here are Margaret and Dinah and Peter, my brothers and sisters in the Lord.'

Heads popped up of what seemed like the entire lay readers' fraternity of St Stephen's. Hands were extended by the men while the women leaned over bags and bundles to press their cheeks to mine. Nick's head turned and he flashed a beaming smile. 'Somewhere in the back, among the suitcases, you will find Pato, my last-born son.'

A boy of about eight suddenly emerged from the boot area to greet us before disappearing again among the assorted luggage. 'Off we go then, my friends!' Nick switched on the engine. 'Say *kwaheri* to your Wilomenah.'

'Just a minute.' A moment's panic made me long, ungratefully, for the safari to be over so that we could be safely back in the flat. 'You did say we'd be back on Thursday evening?'

The plan was that we should return to Nairobi on the long-distance bus, leaving Nick and Alice to complete their vacation. We had therefore told Julius to pick us up from the bus station in the city late on Thursday evening.

Nick nodded, and I prepared to wave to Wilomenah. Then Margaret's head bobbed up again, her face very decisive. 'Friday!' she said.

'We ride the bus home on Friday morning. It will arrive in Nairobi at four in the afternoon.'

Somehow, I put my head out of the half-open window as Nick reversed at top speed. 'Tell Julius Friday!' I called urgently.

Wilomenah's nod was lost in a cloud of exhaust fumes, nudging elbows and crashing suitcases as we took the corner by storm. We travelled a hundred yards and then the car stopped again. 'First we pray,' Nick announced.

We all obediently bowed our heads, and he asked God's help for us on our long safari. Still trying not to think of the practical details of where we were to sleep, I whispered an extra prayer that was to be repeated many times over the next few hours.

The streets of eastern Nairobi were, as usual, choc-a-bloc with traffic, and it took us nearly an hour to forge through the noise, cars and pollution, dropping Annika off at her office on the way. Eventually, however, the mean and crowded streets were replaced with wider avenues flanked with trees, and then it came almost as a shock to realise that we were in open countryside.

It was, in fact, very beautiful countryside, lush and green, with many sights taking our attention and helping us to forget the cramped, uncomfortable conditions in the old car. There were donkeys tethered at the sides of the wide open roads, grazing peacefully, while others pulled carts laden with fruit and vegetables. There were herds of animals, sheep and cattle walking together, herded by whole families.

In the distance, we saw fresh-water lakes as we entered the breathtaking Rift Valley, truly a landscape out of heaven. Here there was abundant fruit for sale, much cleaner and more wholesome looking than in the city. Pears in the high regions, brown and as big and hard as potatoes, pale yellow oranges in the lower regions. The fruit was sold at one home-made stall after another on our route, so that choosing one place to stop and buy seemed virtually impossible. But buy we did, because Margaret insisted, and she and Nick got out of the car at one isolated crossroads to negotiate price and quantity with the eagerly waiting pear sellers. The bargaining took twenty minutes as pears were brought, inspected, given the 'thumbs-down' sign, as sums were mentioned and rejected as being too expensive. We sat patiently, Mark jammed into the front seat with all sorts of paraphernalia around his feet, me easing thankfully but temporarily into the space Margaret had vacated. In the seat behind, Dinah and Peter were elbow to elbow as they endlessly sang choruses together, and in the boot, only the top of young Pato's head was still visible.

'Here, Pato! You take the pears!' Cheerfully, Nick crammed a huge sack into the inches of elastic space. 'Now on with the safari, eh?'

I made myself small again, and we set off, waving to the small multitude of traders who had rushed to our open windows. Wonderful sights were soon flashing before us again—cacti with bright red flowers, people working the land with hand tools reminiscent of medieval England.

Then, as we passed into a stretch of open grassland, we saw them and I leant forward to clasp Mark's arm. 'Look!' I exclaimed delightedly, as I pointed to the wonderful, almost ethereal wild creatures, making their way innocently through the unspoilt landscape. 'Zebra!'

It was the first time either of us had seen zebra except in captivity, and we stared, entranced, at the little flock—a family with young ones following the adults. It was hard to take a photograph in the wildly rocking car, for the road was full of pot-holes. We did our best, and really hoped the photograph would turn out.

We took a short break at the African equivalent of a service station, where food was sold out of doors, and there were, thankfully, very basic toilet facilities. Then we were on our way again, past the salty Lake Elementia in the far distance, covered with a pink hue of flamingoes like the icing on a child's birthday cake.

As we passed into the open countryside again, we saw Masai warriors with their blankets and their cattle. I thought of the night-watchman opposite the flat, and how he often passed his waking hours by having ochre plaited into his long hair by another man. This process took hours and had, I knew, a very important ceremonial place in the story of their culture. It was another example of two worlds uneasily merging, and I marvelled at the African capacity to adjust and survive.

We passed shining peacocks, inches from the road which Nick told us had been built by Italian soldiers during the second world war.

'Some Italian churches were built along the road and they remain today,' he explained, waving a hand airily. 'God travelled with them, you see, as he travels with us today.'

Warmed by this thought, we sat in silence for another hour, while great forests and miles of fertile farmlands rushed past us. Settlements of tin houses on dusty crossroads were called 'towns', and we could hardly believe we had passed through them.

Finally, we came to a junction on the road to Eldoret. 'Here we take the Kisumu road,' Nick said, jamming on the brakes. 'The road to Uganda.'

CHAPTER SIXTEEN

The road ahead was blocked, made impassable by a wide row of double spikes which reminded me of the broken glass on top of our wall at Doonholm. As we drew to a halt, armed soldiers gathered in a cluster around the estate car. One of them, obviously the leader, peered in through the open window at our hot, crushed bodies, his eyes flickering from our white faces to Nick's calm black one above the clerical collar.

'You may go.' The spikes, which I saw were attached to a black rubber barrier bar, were ceremoniously drawn back, snake like, from before our path.

'Just like the children of Israel and the Red Sea, eh?' Our driver joked as he waved to the soldiers and careered us forward on the accelerator. We travelled on, glimpsing for the first time straw-thatched mud huts on the hillsides through the trees. Mark half turned, his eyebrows raised, and we exchanged one of those precious moments of silent telepathy. Would we be sleeping in one of those tonight? Nick still hadn't told us. And if we were in a hut, what would we do about light, and sanitation, and, last but certainly not least, mosquitoes?

Soon we were heading towards Kericho, a

village in the tea-growing area which Margaret told us was famous because it always rained. The countryside here was incredibly green, reminding us of the pictures we saw on tea packets. As we approached, we saw row after row of waist-high, wet-looking tea plants, and, working hard among them, many pickers. They wore identical green-and-yellow-striped tabards, and worked, so Nick told us, many hours in the wet conditions. Nevertheless, their secure jobs were the envy of many because the plantation provided housing, even if only in tin shacks, and basic necessities were all sold at the clearly marked company stores.

'It reminds me of what we've read about the tally shops in Britain in the industrial revolution,' I remarked. I wondered what difficulties these tea workers faced day by day, bound up as they were with a commodity which was in such demand in the affluent West.

Later, we stopped and piled out of the car to stretch our legs. While the rest of the party sang and joked together, we stood and watched Nick and Margaret bargain again with roadside hawkers, this time for six large cabbages and about a stone of potatoes.

'I promised Alice I would bring some food,' Nick explained, as these were dumped on the hardly visible, but still unprotesting Pato. 'There will be many mouths to feed once we all get to Konjra!'

We climbed creakily back aboard and the hot journey began again, taking us on the Kisumu road, and soon, our first sight of sugar plantations and factories. How very rich this beautiful land was, I thought, as I stared out at the fertile plains. And no wonder, as we had been told, that some of the white settlers clung on to their stake in it like grim death when Independence finally came.

'We have rice too,' Nick indicated, as if reading my thoughts a few moments later. 'On the Kumu plain we have many rice fields.'

At Kisumu, Margaret suggested we did a slight detour so that we might be shown Lake Victoria. We drove through the town, recognisably urban, with traffic, an airport, and some quite sophisticated, double-storey shops. Then we turned off the main highway and made our way over rough ground to Heron Point, a beauty spot right on the shore of the vast lake. Here there were many sights which caught our gaze and captured our imaginations, and we tumbled eagerly out of the car again.

As I stood with Mark beneath the trees, watching cattle milling around, I suddenly remembered things I had read about Lake Victoria when I was a young girl, fascinated by Africa. My beloved nan had passed on a big book, bound in dark red leather, *Stanley and Livingstone.* I had pored over the tissue-papered line drawings, seeing Doctor

Livingstone and his colleague with the magnificent Victoria Falls as a backcloth to their meeting: 'Doctor Livingstone, I presume?'

We were, so I understood from Mark, a long way from the Falls. But this *was* the lake, and around it there was much activity. On the shoreline of the blue-grey, lapping water, women sat on the rocks. Mermaid like, their damp *lesos* wrapped around them, they washed the families' clothes by banging them against the stones. Dresses, shirts and underwear festooned the bushes all around them.

There were steamers on the far horizon, and nearer to the shore bobbed fishing and sailing boats. On the water's edge there sat a row of silent, motionless fishermen, their lines hanging straight and limp into the opaque water beneath them. I stood and watched, but none of them seemed to catch anything, their whole demeanour fatalistically patient.

'Carol, my sister.' Nick was suddenly at my side, suggesting brightly: 'Margaret is saying she would like to buy some fish and cook it for you. Is that all right?'

I looked across to where the successful fishermen had their catch of big flat brown fish displayed on the rocks beneath us.

'*Asanta sana*, Margaret,' I called my thanks. 'That would be lovely.'

As she and Nick again went off to bargain, Mark and I exchanged another meaningful glance. 'I hope they're not going to build a fire and cook it here,' I said. 'I don't want to be ungrateful, but time's getting on and we want to be wherever it is we're going before nightfall.'

Margaret beckoned us to where Dinah and Peter had joined in the choosing of our supper. 'These are two fine fat ones,' she said, as two big flat fish were held up for our approval. We nodded, and they were ceremoniously handed to a squatting woman who washed them in the lake and then cleaned them on a rock, her sharp knife making short work of the job.

'Now we get on our way,' Nick decided. He deposited the fish, wrapped in leaves for coolness, in the boot, and we all climbed back in, Pato somehow squeezing into the middle seats between Margaret and myself.

'I think you had better do that, little Pato!' Margaret beamed, slapping and then shaking his hand. 'We still have to stop to buy bananas!'

CHAPTER SEVENTEEN

'In an hour or two we will reach Agunja!' breathed Nick, as we braked at a dusty crossroads. 'From there it is only fifty kilometres to my home. But first, we drop Dinah and Peter. They have relatives here.'

Dinah and Peter climbed out of the sweltering car, retrieving their luggage from the bulging boot. 'They will join us at Konjra tomorrow,' Nick explained, taking off again in a cloud of dust. 'Then we will continue to praise the Lord together.'

At my side, Margaret began to sing another chorus, the irresistible rhythm and Swahili words soon catching all our voices. As the afternoon wore on, and the miles seemed never ending, Mark turned and met my eyes in another moment of perfect understanding. I knew that, like me, he had forgotten the worry about where we were going to spend the night. We just wanted to reach our destination. Any destination.

To our dismay, though, Nick did not carry on through the landmark that was Agunja. He stopped right outside an old western-style bar, parking the car in the full glare of the sun.

'Here we must find the carpenter,' he said to my total amazement.

'Carpenter?' Again, Mark's head came round, while Nick smiled brightly from one to the other of us.

'For the church doors, my friends,' he explained, as if it were perfectly obvious. 'Come, Margaret. We will not be long.'

A moment later, he and Margaret disappeared into the shimmering heat and dust, leaving us marooned in what felt like a sea of staring brown eyes. The eyes came from all directions, the makeshift stalls set up along the dirt road, the people passing to and from the bar. Endless ragged, barefoot children who walked by with the chickens clucking around their heels.

'They have not seen *wuzungu* before,' Pato explained matter of factly. He yawned and stretched and climbed out of the car, looking for a cool spot under the nearest tree. Meanwhile, the attention we were creating was increasing by the minute. As we sat there, feeling like exhibits in a cage, a drunk with glazed eyes shuffled over from the bar. He stood swaying, inches from the window, staring and mumbling.

'Sorry, we don't speak Swahili,' Mark said as the drunk came closer, repeating his request.

'Luo,' Pato corrected from under the tree. As the man held out an unsteady hand, he explained. 'He's asking for money. But if you give it to him, he will go back into the bar and others will follow.'

Feeling even more exposed, we guiltily took the line of least resistance. 'Sorry,' Mark said, 'we do not have money.'

The man shuffled and muttered, hesitated, tried once more then finally gave up, weaving his way back to the shelter of the bar.

Where *was* Nick? As a group of small children pressed against the other windows, pointing and nodding towards us, I looked helplessly around. The town seemed to be built around a dilapidated market, open air and rambling, with piles of tiny dried smoked fish spread everywhere. Women sat among the piles, holding empty margarine containers to be used as scoops. There was the customary sight of goats feeding on garbage, and the passing traffic of women and small children acting as beasts of burden.

A bus suddenly drew to a halt like an old-fashioned stage coach, causing a flurry of dust. People descended on it like buzzards, unloading, loading, using all the time and energy available. Soon it was unrecognisable under sacks of vegetables and grain, and huge bunches of green bananas still attached to their stems. All being borne by human and animal freight. It disappeared, tilting and rocking, in a cacophony of screeches, along the road to Uganda.

Meanwhile it was four o'clock, and there was still no sign of our leader. We had given up, and were miserably sunk into the sticky seats, cringing away from the staring eyes, when the sound of Nick's welcome laughter echoed, and he was there, Margaret at his side.

'Sorry, sorry,' he said as he climbed back into the driver's seat. 'The carpenter was not there, and so we had to find him. And in finding him, I met many old friends.'

In Africa, he explained, as he reversed and swiftly took us out of Agunja, if you are going to catch a train and you meet a friend, it is more important that you stop and talk to the friend. There will always be another train, and friends are more important than safaris.

'But what about the church doors?' I asked before I could stop myself. 'Is he able to fit them?'

'He will come to my place tomorrow, my sister,' Nick said. 'By tomorrow our church will have its very own doors!'

By tomorrow, I thought, we would—presumably—be in Konjra. We would know where we were going to stay and how we would be spending the two days until the official opening and consecration of St Mark's church.

As the scenery grew denser and the mud huts more prominent amid the distant hills, I thought wistfully of our flat, far away in comfortable Nairobi. We had long since left the road, and we bumped along on wide mud tracks full of enormous pot-holes which Nick managed to avoid. To our eyes it seemed like a landscape straight out of the Old Testament, a landscape full of walkers, from tiny children to elderly men and women. Mostly barefoot, mostly burdened by water containers of bananas or armfuls of man-sized sugar cane. All had one thing in common—the fact that they were travelling.

'Here in Konjra, there are no *matatu*. We must walk everywhere,' Nick explained. 'For water, for food, for school. When I was a boy, I walked seven miles to school without shoes, and seven miles back each day.'

Beside the tracks was green bush out of which would suddenly pop dark heads. Sometimes whole groups of children would spot our white faces and wave and cheer wildly, breaking into a run after the car.

'*Wuzungu!*'

'*Jambo!*' We waved back, delighted. As we moved deeper into the bush, drawing towards our destination, we were gratified to realise that many of the people we passed seemed to know Nick and almost to be expecting him.

'This is our land,' Nick explained as the countryside opened into a green vista dotted with huts. 'My family has farmed here for many generations. This is the home of my ancestors and the place where my heart will always be. It has been a long safari, but it is nearly over now, my friends. We will go to my house where Alice will be waiting to greet you and to make you welcome. But first, I will show you our church of St Mark's.'

We drove along a bumpy path which at first sight seemed too narrow for a vehicle. Again, we glimpsed huts half hidden in clearings, saw and smelt smoke and livestock. Looking across the expanse of greenery, we saw banana groves laden with fruit. Suddenly, we veered round a corner, went up a slope and found ourselves in another clearing. A large building stood there, built of brick blocks. There was a richness in its rusty brown colour. It was only half completed, but its very newness was both a challenge and a witness to the living God.

'Welcome to St Mark's, Konjra,' said Nick, as he opened the car doors and let us out. Wonderingly, we followed him across the grass and through the gaping doorway into a blissfully cool interior. It had the same name, and was to be dedicated to the same saint as my home church. That, I told myself as I looked around, was the reason behind the 'God-incidences' that had brought me here. That was all. And yet, scarcely able to breathe, I gripped Mark's hand as the amazing revelation hit me. I was in a strange, half-built church in the middle of rural East Africa, continents away from everything and everyone I knew and loved. Yet, amazingly, I felt as if I had just come home!

CHAPTER EIGHTEEN

We left the church just as darkness fell over the lush green bush, insects buzzing in the warm air around us. The whole world seemed hushed and full of expectation. Another group of Konjra children had gathered to watch us both enter and leave the uncompleted building. As we walked the few yards back to the still loaded car, they followed, wide eyed and barefooted. They were very thin by western standards and dressed in an assortment of clothes that obviously came from another culture, faded hand-me-down dresses and T-shirts that were no longer fashionable in Europe.

We called, '*Kwaheri*, goodbye,' as we were again jolted into motion, and the children ran alongside the car until the speed left them behind.

'Here we are then,' Nick suddenly manoeuvred the car into another clearing through a set of wooden gates. Then he stopped and put on the handbrake. 'Home!' he breathed in satisfaction.

As Margaret and Pato got out, Mark and I looked about us. Behind the trees we could see more huts, but the house in the compound in front of us was entirely different. A long, low building of one storey, it was constructed of the same rusty coloured stone as St Mark's church.

'*Karibu*, my dear friends. This is where you will stay as our honoured guests!' Nick announced. He clapped his hands and within seconds the path leading up to the house, under the shadow of the garage, seemed to be thronged with people. 'These are all our friends in the Lord who work and stay here.' Our host went on as they lined up in two almost deferential rows to shake hands with us. 'They too wish to welcome you. And here is

94

my beloved Alice.'

Nick's wife bustled out of the house wearing a headscarf and a brightly coloured *leso* and enfolded me in a hug. 'You have had a long, long journey, eh?' she said rhetorically. 'But never mind. Praise the Lord you are here! You rest now.'

Gratefully, we took our bag and mosquito net and followed her indoors. An oblong room greeted us, filled with comfortable armchairs and sofas. At one end stood a big, family-sized table covered in a snowy white cloth and holding an oil lamp.

'I am sorry to say we have no electricity or indoor plumbing here,' Nick explained as we all sat down and automatically kicked off our shoes. 'But we have a generator and oil lamps, and the earth privy is outside.'

In spite of myself, my heart sank and I had another pang of longing for the flat at Doonholm, where at least there was a flushable loo! Then Alice came in and I forgot my unease at the brightness of her smile.

'Let me show you to your room. We have already drawn the blinds against the mosquitoes.'

The room, lit by another oil lamp, was large and comfortable, with floor-to-ceiling windows which overlooked the pitch-black garden. As we unpacked, a tap came at the door and Pato came in. He had a struggling and squawking white chicken under his arm. 'A present,' he

95

said.

I stared, nonplussed, at the chicken. Pato laughed. 'The chicken is for dinner,' he said. 'This is for you!' Carefully, he took a small, self-adhesive plastic hook from his pocket and, with his free hand, attached it to the wall at the side of the double bed. 'For your clothes.'

As people came in to erect our mosquito net, Nick called us back into the sitting room where we were served with hot tea and margarine sandwiches. 'When you are rested, I will show you around,' he said. 'The best cure for sitting so many hours on safari is to take another safari—on foot!'

We needed our torches as, later on, we stepped outside the house. We found immediately that Nick was right. It *was* good to walk, particularly in such cool evening air and under the light of such stars. We realised, not for the first time, how much we missed the simple exercise and freedom of going out on foot. It was a luxury we were denied on both the crowded, dangerous streets of Nairobi and the building site around Doonholm.

'You see that big tree?' Nick stopped and pointed across the garden. 'That is a sycamore fig tree, like the one climbed by the tax collector, Zacchaeus. It is a sacred tree. The tree next to it is sacred also, because my grandfather is buried beneath it.'

'But the sycamore?' I stared at the giant, ghost-like outline of twisted branches and low, sprawling trunk. You could indeed imagine a small man being able to climb easily into its dark and cosy lap.

'Ah, my sister.' Even in the half light, the look of soft reminiscence was clearly visible on Nick's face. 'The vision for St Mark's church was born under that tree. My father, who was the local priest, and his Christian friends stood under it and prayed and praised the Lord and made that tree their church.'

As we too moved beneath the boughs of the great sycamore, Nick went on: 'St Mark's was here for a long, long time in spirit, but without structure. The structure was my father's dream, and it has become my dream. Now you can see the results, up there on the hillside.'

'So the consecration of St Mark's has been a long time coming?' I said thoughtfully. Into my mind's eye came the image of my own church in the West Midlands. 'Our' St Mark's had been built thanks to the benevolence of a local earl. Though now as much the worse for wear as any other Victorian church, it still possessed the basic requirements of a completed roof, and doors and windows. As far as I could see, St Mark's Konjra would be consecrated in its half-completed state, a fact which, in this environment, was obviously not important.

'Tomorrow, I will show you around the village properly,' our host said warmly. 'My father's grave, the river, the people in the compound. There is much to see, but it is too dark now, and we must be careful of the mosquitoes. Now we should go back to the house for supper and prayers.'

Supper was laid on the big, sitting-room table, and people of all ages and both sexes came from all over the house to eat or serve or work in the lamplit kitchen. There was another, smaller table in the kitchen which was also soon filled. We gave thanks and then eagerly tucked into rice, chicken stew and chapatis. Trying not to remember the squawking bundle I'd seen earlier under Pato's arm, I concentrated on spooning sauce onto my plate. After supper, we all sat down on the sofas again and the worship began. We sang choruses and old hymns, and had prayers, the family gathering round us out of the shadows of the house.

'These are my sisters, my *big* sisters!' Nick introduced three enormous, grinning African ladies in headscarves and *lesos*. 'And this is my aunt, the sister of my late father. She is wanting very much to meet you people.'

An old, old woman extended her hand. '*Jambo! Habare*?' she cackled delightedly as she took our hands. Then she promptly sat down on the floor.

'My aunt does not like chairs,' Nick explained as we looked at each other in surprise. 'She likes to sit on the earth, beneath the banana tree. And to walk. She has walked many kilometres to be with us today.'

He translated his words into the local language and the old lady nodded vigorously, grinning toothlessly up at us. Nick, meanwhile, stretched out his stockinged feet. 'Now, sister Carol, perhaps you would like to share something with us. Then my brother Mark can lead us in prayer before we all look for our beds.'

I took a deep breath. There seemed only one possible story I could share. The one I had already spoken of in St Stephen's and other Nairobi churches, about how the Lord had called me over some many years to come to Africa, to work and minister at the Metropolitan Hospital. Nick translated my words into Swahili and then Alice translated the Swahili into Luo. Everyone listened intently, the silence broken only when I had finished by suitably exuberant cries: '*Bwana asifiwe!*' Praise God!'

The testimony and its response led straight into Mark's prayers of thanksgiving for our safe journey and warm welcome. He asked a blessing on Nick's house and all who lived and shared and worshipped the Lord here.

Instead of turning in for the night, however, we stayed up for ages, singing and praising in the words of the melodic Swahili choruses we were beginning at last to recognise and understand. The singing led naturally to clapping and the clapping to swaying and dancing, so that eventually we were all dancing around the dimly lit, comfortable sitting room.

'It's wonderful here!' I said to Mark as we later braved the outside earth privy and then climbed into bed. 'And to think we were worried we might be sleeping in a mud hut being eaten alive by malarious mosquitoes!'

'There don't seem to be any mosquitoes,' Mark said, yawning, as he turned off the oil lamp and got in beside me. 'Strange, after what Nick said I expected quite a few of them.'

Relieved and exhausted, we drifted off to sleep. It wasn't until next morning, when Pato came in to bring our hot water, that we discovered we'd had an overnight guest.

'Look!' the boy cried delightedly, pointing to a pale, elegant green shadow on the bedroom wall—a shadow which disappeared immediately between the wall cracks. 'My father says God made those lizards to bless us. Their favourite food is the mosquito.'

CHAPTER NINETEEN

We had been woken by the sound of laughter and voices raised in song. After washing and dressing, we went out to join the assembled company in the sitting room.

'Today, many more friends will come to fellowship with us,' Nick prophesied happily. 'We will all be preparing for the consecration of our church, an occasion which the Lord has made even more special by bringing you people to us.'

After a breakfast of bread, fried eggs and boiled green bananas, we had a time of prayer in which all the household took part. 'Now I will show you round,' our host decided. 'First, we will go into the garden.'

In the garden there was much activity: young women cleaning pots and pans, or washing clothes by hand as Wilomenah did; older women, including Nick's sister and aunt, sitting on the ground in the shade of the trees. We exchanged greetings with them all. Then people began to arrive, some carrying live chickens in shopping baskets, others with bunches of bananas or pawpaws on their heads. Behind the gates, groups of children wandered, peeping curiously in at our white faces, waving and laughing, and disappearing again.

Margaret, Alice and Pato came out of the house and stood under the holy sycamore tree, beginning to sing, clap and sway. The words of the Swahili choruses were complicated but as always the actions were simple, repetitive and irresistible. We joined in, thoroughly enjoying ourselves, with seemingly endless time to perfect them. With every verse, another person joined in so that soon the whole household was assembled for more impromptu worship.

'Ah, here is my brother, Jonah!' Nick

suddenly announced, as a tall African in a worn but neat suit came into the compound. 'He will accompany us on the sightseeing!'

Soon, the four of us were setting off on foot through the gates and onto the straight, wide path which led to the church. 'My name is Jonah Aringo, and I love the Lord Jesus!' Nick's brother began as we fell into step. 'I am the co-ordinator of the family relief project here.'

Jonah went on to explain that the project dispensed aid from overseas to needy rural children and their families. There was a primary school, a scheme to encourage communal food growing, and a dispensary which so far had no medical supplies.

'Pity there isn't a Metropolitan hospital nearby,' I said to Mark, thinking of the now flourishing project God had led us to back in Nairobi.

'The nearest hospital to Konjra is forty kilometres, my sister,' Nick said, overhearing. 'And the only transport is the church taxi—the bicycle which collects our visitors from Kisumu.'

We had neared the church now, its cool, open exterior drawing me like a magnet. We went inside, stopping to pray in the open-ended crossing, and I felt again the hope and excitement that the Holy Spirit seemed to inspire in me in that particular place.

'Come and see the project office,' Jonah

invited, when we stepped back into the open air. 'You can see some of our children.'

He led us to a neat, one-storey building behind the church. Inside was a wall completely covered in photographs. 'We have sponsors from America and the UK,' he said. 'Without them, the children here would receive no education, because their parents have only what they can grow in the ground.'

We walked a mile or so further into the lush green bush until we reached a clearing full of workers. 'This is our *shamba* or field,' Jonah explained as we stood watching the women and children at work with handheld tools. 'The project provides the seeds and we provide the labour. That way, everyone benefits. Thanks to overseas aid, wells have been sunk too, so that water is available to everyone at a distance of only three or four kilometres from their homes.'

Next we were taken to the primary school— a series of mud buildings, some without a roof. We met the hard-working principal who was delighted to see us, pressing us to sign his visitors' book.

'We do not get many visitors,' he explained as he dug into a dusty cupboard and emerged clutching the thin red book. 'Your names will be a source of great pride to us.'

We were shown around to classrooms where barefoot children sat on the mud floor, listening to a teacher who had little or no equipment. Where there were desks, they were ancient cast-offs from the British educational system of the 1940s and 1950s. Slates and chalks were also in use, taking us back even further to the previous century.

'Many of the children in the rural parts of Kenya never get to complete their education,' Nick told us as we made our way back towards his home. 'And even if they do manage to get to secondary school, there is nothing for them except to go to the city where life is cheap and only the most highly qualified find worthwhile employment. In many cases it is safer to stay in one's home and grow maize and try to buy a goat or two. But as you will know, young people do not always want to be safe, and for many the old ways have little or no attraction.'

On the way back to the house, he took us on a detour to show us a typical polygamous family group.

'Here is the first hut,' he explained, stopping to speak to a smiling, toothless man who sat on the ground in front of it. 'This is the father's house. And these three huts you see around are for each of his three wives.'

The huts were built around a clearing, where a woman sat cooking over an open fire. She was occasionally brought provisions by other *leso*-dressed women, all of whom stopped to speak and laugh with her. In between the huts, small children played and slightly bigger ones worked, digging or laying out wet clothes to dry on rocks and bushes. Counting huts, I pointed out, 'There are six huts. Who do the others belong to?'

This time, Jonah answered, nodding towards the cluster of tall young men who appeared from between the trees. 'Each son, when he reaches manhood, is given his own hut. The family builds it for him with mud and grass.'

'Cheaper than shelling out for a bachelor flat I suppose,' Mark smiled, thinking no doubt of Edmund back home.

We went cheerfully back to Nick's feeling that we had learnt a lot about daily life in Konjra. Little did we realise how much more there was waiting—just around the corner.

CHAPTER TWENTY

'Ah, Carol! Mark! We have missed you!' It was the next afternoon when Dinah and Peter emerged, blinking, from the car that belonged to the Agunja carpenter.

'The Lord is so good!' Peter marvelled as the welcoming group in the garden came over to greet them. 'We were left by the *akamba* bus and then Dennis here found us.'

'I was on my way to fit your doors, brother Nick,' the beaming carpenter explained. 'I knew these people must belong to you. And so

I bring them.'

'*Asante sana*, my friend!' Nick grinned. Turning to Mark and myself he said, 'You see, my sister and brother, in Africa it is always good to stop for a friend.'

After Dennis, Dinah and Peter had been served refreshments, the carpenter went off to look at the church. Nick suggested that we take a drive to the river. 'It is too far for you people to walk,' he said with a rueful grin, 'but I would like you to see it. The river is at the heart of our life here in Konjra.'

Soon we were bumping over the roughest terrain we had ever seen, our route taking us along narrow, winding paths, up the sides of miniature mountains and across cracks and ravines that plunged half the road into craters. The car was full again, and we swayed and clutched each other as Nick expertly manoeuvred us on our way. Leaving the road altogether, we eventually found ourselves bumping precariously across open land, stopping on the edge of a muddy slope which fell straight into the water.

'When I was a boy, I fished here for food, upstream, where the little fishes come,' Nick reminisced as we all climbed out of the vehicle. 'There are many, many thousands of tiny fishes, a rich source of protein. They are dried and sold cheaply in the market place at Agunja. The Lord is so good because the fishes are so easy to catch. You just open your

106

net, or even your hand, and they swim right inside!'

Across the clear surface of the still water, a long, low canoe was gliding towards us, paddled gracefully by one young African while another sat in the stern. 'Here is our transport!' Nick exclaimed. 'Shall we take a trip to the other side and back?'

To my surprise, jolly Dinah drew back, shaking her head. 'Not me, brother Nick!' she said firmly. 'I stay with the car. I do not like the water.'

Her confession was met by bursts of good-natured laughter and teasing.

'Oh Dinah, where is your faith?'

'Come on, sister Dinah—just a little ride on the lovely river!'

'You will not drown! We promise you!'

But Dinah, though smiling, resolutely turned away, only waving when we were all in the canoe and about to leave the shore.

'Here, this boat is very special, my friends!' Nick called, as the two young sailors nodded and grinned, saying something to him in Luo. 'As you can see, it offers several grades of transport.'

Puzzled, we followed his pointing finger to the seats on which we sat. Painted boldly on the sides were the words 'first class', 'second class' and 'third class'. We joked about who was sitting where until Margaret, who was in 'first class' said she might as well pretend to be a lady and trail her hand in the water.

Immediately, the young man in the stern caught at her arm, his expression very serious. 'Please, madam,' he said. 'No fingers in the water. They will attract the water snakes!'

We all drew a little closer to each other after that, keeping our eyes warily on the undisturbed surface of the clear, grey water.

'Looks like there's another passenger waiting,' Mark pointed out as the boat drew alongside the far shore. A middle-aged woman stepped carefully aboard, carrying bundles of *leso*-wrapped goods.

'She is taking them to sell at the market,' Nick explained as we listened to her negotiating in her own language with the canoeist. 'She is telling him she will pay in bananas.'

When we eventually returned to our embarkation point, and the waiting car, the woman silently dropped a bunch of tiny, pale yellow bananas onto the 'third-class' seat of the canoe.

'Payment in kind is fine,' Jonah explained from the 'second-class' seat before we followed the woman up the muddy bank. 'The canoe does a great trade, taking people and even their cattle across the river.'

'The cattle swim, of course, my sister,' Nick rejoined as we shook hands with the boatmen and went back to Dinah and the car. 'Now we will take the car home, then before we have supper, I promised I would show you my father's grave.'

Within the hour, we found ourselves on another seemingly endless trail that was full of pedestrians. It was amazing that people all had somewhere to go, so purposeful and yet so relaxed, always ready to stop and shake hands and pass the time of day. We watched the children, some little more than eight years old, fetching water, digging in the earth, sitting at the roadside with a display of fruit in front of them. Many chewed on raw sugar cane as they went about their business, tearing at the green stalks with their strong, white teeth, and extracting the sweetness from inside.

We passed members of religious communities, notably the white-clad Legio Maria, and groups of school children in formal brown or green uniforms, following, barefoot, after quiet-faced, black nuns. All stopped to speak with us, intrigued by our *wuzungu* faces, interested when Nick told them where we were from and what we did there.

'*Bwana asifiwe!*' We were beginning to say it too, and they threw back their heads and laughed, clapping their hands against ours in delight that we too could praise the Lord in Swahili.

We walked off the main track, down pathways buzzing with insects, undergrowth brushing our hands and faces. Finally we reached a hidden clearing in which stood a hut, made, like the others we had seen, of thick mud, but different in that it was square shaped.

'This was my father's house,' Nick said proudly, and, indicating the healthy looking livestock in the clearing in front of it, 'These cattle belong to my stepmother, his second wife.'

He led us up to the doorway of the primitive building, and then pointed to the ground in front of the entrance. 'Here is my mother's grinding stone, where she ground the maize and millet for many years before she died. As you can see, the stone is very, very smooth. And here, next to it, by his front door, is my father's grave.'

We stared at the unfamiliar sight, the almost western-style grave, oblong in shape, with a plain stone cross at its head. It was as if Nick's late father still stood guard over the entrance to his home in order to watch over his family.

'Come inside,' our host invited as he led us through the door. 'You cannot go back to England without going into a real African home.'

I blinked as I followed Mark and the others into the dim interior. I had the impression of coolness and depth, of earth and security. It was like entering a windowless cave. It was a cave filled with chairs. Around its square sides were wooden chairs of every size and shape, providing seating for a large family, and showing up almost ghost like in the light of a single oil lamp. The lamp stood on a table near the entrance, its inefficient light spilling onto a school exercise book at its side. A boy of about eleven sat at the table, poring over the book, while a smaller child played in the dust on the floor, and an old woman, materialising out of the cool darkness, came from an inner chamber to extend a flat, dry hand.

'This is my stepmother, Matilda,' Nick introduced. 'She stays here and takes care of her great grandchildren, and tends my father's grave. She says she praises God that you have come to visit us, and is looking forward to sharing in the celebration of the opening of our church.'

'Tell her we're looking forward to that too,' I replied. As we turned to leave the mud home, I thought suddenly of Dennis, the carpenter. I wondered, fleetingly, if St Mark's had those doors fitted yet.

CHAPTER TWENTY-ONE

'Now all we need are the windows!' Nick pointed out as we stood before the great, acacia-wood doors. The women of the village had been working all day, cleaning up after the carpenter and washing the cement floor with bucket after bucket of cold water. An assortment of benches had been carried in, although it was clear that most of the congregation would have to sit on the floor.

'Tomorrow we will bring the furniture for the chancel,' Sister Sarah, a blue-robed lay reader said. 'And the balloons and streamers for the decorating. My sisters in the Mothers' Union will be preparing the food.'

'So what's new?' I grinned, meeting Mark's eyes. Like many other Mothers' Union branches in England, St Mark's, Pensnett, could always be called upon to provide refreshments, particularly for a special occasion.

'Somehow I don't think you'll find the old bourbon biscuits on this menu,' Mark replied meaningfully, 'especially if the bishop, archdeacon and rural dean are expected.'

Nick assured us solemnly that their dignitaries were indeed coming to take part in the consecration and official opening of St Mark's. 'With no telephone here, and the roads impassable in times of heavy rain, we have to trust them to the Lord,' he said calmly. 'But I have no doubt that they will be here.'

Leaving the church half full of helpers, we went out to the project office. After prayer and discussion, we had decided to sponsor an orphan, a boy of three, whom Jonah had pointed out to us the day before.

'His name is Richard,' he'd explained, as the

112

small, solemn figure gravely shook hands with us both. 'Before she died, his mother suffered from a disease which affected her mind. After the father deserted the family, she used to leave Richard out in the bush in the middle of the night. It was only the Lord who saved him from being killed by wild animals.'

Richard's father was now also dead, and so the boy was cared for by his extended family. It would be good, I thought, and worthwhile, for us to sponsor him as a family. As we gave Jonah and a social worker our address and other details, I suddenly couldn't wait to tell Sarah and the boys about their brand-new brother!

'Obviously another reason why God brought us to Africa,' Mark said as we later went for what had become a regular late afternoon walk with Nick and Alice. This time we seemed to go right into the heart of the bush, past huts which were basic and hidden from view, past sellers of sugar cane and harvesters of maize, bent double with their wares. Small, ragged carriers passed us one after another, some carrying petrol cans full of drinking water on their heads.

'Don't they realise the dangers of lead poisoning?' I asked, horrified.

Nick shook his head. 'Many things in the West are taken for granted,' he said, 'but people here really do not know that contaminated water can be dangerous. We still have typhoid because it is not known that water should be boiled and not taken from near latrines.'

We walked on in a kind of sweet fellowship that for me heightened all perceptions. Never before had I been so aware of God's beautiful, multifarious world around us, given as such a generous gift to each and every one of us. Standing on a sloping hillside, Nick showed us the vast expanse of land owned by his ancestors, stretching off to the distant horizon. 'You see the bushland over there? That is where I used to go when I walked to school, my friends.'

We shook our heads, wondering at the sheer distance. Nick shook his too, but for a different reason. 'Now, because of school fees, many children cannot go to school, no matter how far they are prepared to walk. I am very lucky, because without my education, I would still be grazing goats.'

Thoughtfully, we turned and began to retrace our steps on the long way home. Darkness pressed about us, yet the journeying figures on the dirt roads were no fewer. Seeing how small some of the unaccompanied children were, I couldn't help but compare this to England where nowadays many parents would be afraid to allow their children such freedom. Here the dangers were obviously not from abductors and abusers but from poverty, ignorance and disease.

Turning a corner, we passed a tiny stall, half hidden in the undergrowth and made entirely from an overturned wooden box. *'Jambo!'* we stopped and shook hands with the teenaged girl who stood alone behind it.

'Here is your local supermarket, my sister,' Nick joked. He introduced us to the girl. 'These people are two pastors from England.'

I looked down at the stall, seeing the usual pitiful assortment of items: candles, matches, pencil stubs, a block of Kimbo cooking fat, cut into two-ounce pieces. Just then a small boy appeared at my elbow. Holding out a coin, he pointed to the fat. The girl took his money and wrapped the precious square of Kimbo in a piece of newspaper she took from a dusty cardboard box at the back of the stall. Mosquitoes buzzed around our heads.

'Don't go yet, *bwana!*' As we prepared to leave, the girl held up a restraining hand and turned back to the box. To my surprise, she took from it a battered Bible and a piece of paper.

'You may be able to help me,' she said. 'All day I have been looking for a quotation. It is for my Sunday school test.'

In the fading light, we peered at the pencilled question. 'Where is it that Jesus says, "In heaven, their angels always see the face of my father who is in heaven?"'

At my side, Mark smiled. 'That's Matthew chapter eighteen, verse ten.' Reaching across, he took the Bible and turned its pages on the dirty stall. 'There, look, it's where he's talking to the disciples about not despising the little children.'

'Oh yes!' The girl's face relaxed. Taking a stub of pencil from the box, she wrote the reference laboriously on her test paper. 'Thank you!' she smiled, shaking our hands again. 'I had given up being able to find it. *'Bwana asifiwe!'*

'Bwana asifiwe!' The four of us called in unison and turned, waving, to go on our way. As we did so, I suddenly became aware of another group of trudging people, only half visible on the other side of the broad, pot-holed path. A woman, accompanied by several children, was walking on her way to some unknown bushland destination. As Nick called out a greeting to her, she stopped, and the eldest child, a girl who looked about eight years old, stopped too. Her left leg was extended painfully in front of her, and blood and pus was running down over it onto her filthy, bare foot. 'What have you done?' Imagining it to be the result of some recent fall or accident, I hurried to her side.

The child just looked at me, her dark eyes mute and full of suffering like those of a hurt animal. I turned to Jonah. 'Ask her mother how she has done this!' I requested. Looking down at her leg, I saw a huge, livid wound, open to the bone, stretching from her knee all

116

down her shin bone. Jonah spoke quickly to the woman who was staring suspiciously at us, her three other children clinging to her skirts. She replied sullenly, and after a moment's conversation, Jonah told me, 'She says it just came. She says the child has seen a doctor, but it gets no better.'

I knew nothing about medicine, and had not even done a first-aid course, but even I knew that the wound needed urgent dressing, and above all, rest.

'Sometimes these things are a result of malnutrition,' Nick explained as the woman, indicating the child to walk ahead, slid away into the darkness. 'A simple bite or burn, when the body has no resistance and conditions are unhygienic, can turn into a killer.'

We carried on home, silenced by what we had seen. I couldn't get the sight of it out of my mind, the impact of that silent suffering out of my heart. When we at last reached the house, and Nick and Jonah led the way, Mark turned to me. 'Strange,' he mused, 'about that Scripture reading. It came just before you turned and saw her.'

'Jonah!' How slow we are sometimes, and how tired God our Father must get of nudging us into action! I caught up with the project leader just before he disappeared inside. 'We must find out who that little girl is!' I urged, suddenly realising just how important it was. 'Will you promise to find her for me tomorrow?'

CHAPTER TWENTY-TWO

'What's that noise?' Over and above the raging, tropical thunderstorm came the sound of a voice. Mark and I listened, cocooned beneath our mosquito net, still reeling from the ferocious bursts of thunder and lightning flashes which had woken us. The whole earth seemed to be shaking as the rain flooded down, its heavy, drenching intensity like nothing we had ever experienced in England. The voice went higher, moaning and wailing in prayer, placated by another, calmer voice, that of Margaret, lay reader and fellow passenger on our safari here.

'It's Dinah!' Mark whispered as we exchanged nervous smiles. 'She's praying out loud.'

'This must be even worse than going in a boat, if you're scared of thunder,' I said thoughtfully. As another thunder clap burst overhead, I tried to imagine what it must be like spending such a night in one of those mud-and-thatch huts in the compounds we had seen.

By morning, however, the storm was just a memory, and we emerged, blinking, from Nick's house to a bright and clean new day—

the day St Mark's, Konjra was to be consecrated for the worship of the Lord. Dinah goodnaturedly laughed off the teasing she had no doubt expected about the night before, and joined us under the sycamore tree. 'The service should begin at ten,' Nick replied in answer to my question. 'But first we must welcome all our visitors and wait for the bishop and the rural dean.'

'While we wait, we will praise the Lord!' Margaret said happily. 'We should begin our singing in preparation. We began to sing our Swahili choruses, swaying and clapping, repeating the words over and over again, led by first one resonant solo voice and then another.

'I know!' I said, as Peter and Dinah gave a cheer. 'Today we'll be the new international singing and dancing choir. After all, Mark's American, I'm English and you're all Kenyan.'

Once we had decided that we were a choir, it seemed all the more important that we should practise, and gradually we were joined by other voices. Neighbours, bringing food for the post-festival meal, would sway over the grass, encouraged by the music. Girls coming out to wash clothes or fetch water would delay the task in hand so that they too could spend a little time just praising the Lord.

At ten minutes past ten, Nick jumped into his car, saying he would go and look for the bishop. 'He has many kilometres to travel. I

119

will perhaps meet him on the road and save his feet.'

He returned about twenty minutes later with three beaming clergymen in the back of the vehicle. As they climbed out, each introduced himself before being taken indoors by Alice.

'So now we have the bishop, archdeacon and rural dean,' Peter said in satisfaction. 'The service will soon begin.'

'*Pole, pole*, my brother! Slowly, slowly!' Nick insisted through delighted chuckles. 'First they must eat breakfast. The bananas are just being cooked.'

At 11.30 we arrived at St Mark's, Konjra for its official opening and consecration. The window spaces in the building shell were decorated with streamers and balloons. In the chancel area stood a scrubbed kitchen table and in front of it an old hearthrug. Chairs had been placed in the sanctuary, and in front of them, as impromptu hassocks, were pillows off people's beds. The building was half full of people, many of them swaying and singing. An air of expectancy hung over the whole proceedings as we waited in the half-built vestry. Outside in the sunshine, the uniformed Mothers' Union and lay readers from St Stephen's and St Mark's made their own procession.

'As we prepare for our worship, let us remember we are here to give thanks to God for the gift of this church of St Mark.' The bishop looked from one to another of us as we assembled before him. 'In giving thanks, my brothers and sisters, we must also remember how privileged we are to have with us our guests, ministers from England.'

He nodded graciously to us. 'I understand that our sister here is also serving at St Mark's—St Mark's, England,' he went on. 'And I have just learnt that her husband, the Methodist minister, is called Mark!'

There was a buzz of interest and approval from the waiting procession. It lifted into a deafening cheer as the bishop went on enthusiastically: 'As she is from St Mark's, and he is called Mark, we shall call them the two Marks. And we shall ask our brother Mark to kindly preach the sermon at today's celebration.'

'Yes, my brother!' the exuberant archdeacon put in, as Mark's mouth dropped open. 'The Lord has surely given you a word for us today.'

In a daze we entered the church with its patiently waiting congregation. We sang, as we moved, an old Moody and Sankey hymn in Swahili, Luo and English, our combined voices raised in a cacophony of praise. As we walked down the aisle, I noticed that many children were there, standing holding baby brothers and sisters in their arms. Some were scarcely more than six years old. The hymn ended and the call to worship began, and they sat gracefully on the floor, their charges climbing into their small, open arms to go to sleep.

As the service got underway we realised that this was going to be a mammoth session. Not only was there to be the consecration by the bishop, there were prayers, greetings and homilies from the archdeacon and rural dean in between the enthusiastic praising. The new international singing and dancing choir performed. Then the Sunday school danced, tiny girls in *lesos*, with one leading singer and a drum for accompaniment. Sarah, the lay reader, gave a testimony, and Nick, with the air of one retelling a story that was part of him, talked about the sycamore tree and his father's vision. 'Visions, dreams and angels. That is what the Christian life is about, my friends,' he said. 'But it's also about practical help, and that is why, before the end of this holy service, we shall have a *harambee*. But first, I am going to ask our brother Mark from England to give us the message the Lord has entrusted to him today.'

'Good luck, darling!' I whispered, squeezing Mark's hand as he got up to go to the lectern, carried by singing voices from all around. But as I looked at him, ready to speak, an interpreter on either side, I knew neither of us had any need to worry. Thanks to the presence of God the Holy Spirit, whatever he had to say, however impromptu, would be exactly what the people needed to hear.

The service finished at 3 pm with what was for me an indescribably meaningful moment. In wonderful, soaring Swahili, the choir led our recessional hymn, 'God be with you till we meet again'. As I joined in the procession, I could hardly sing for the lump in my throat or see through the tears in my eyes. For although the choirmaster here could not possibly have known it, this was a special favourite at St Mark's, Pensnett, one which our smaller, less exotic choir sang at every important church occasion.

Outside, as the procession was blessed and dismissed, Mark and I stood with the dignitaries and shook hands with the people streaming out. Each one said, *'Bwana asifiwe!'* or simply, 'Amen!' This was an affirmation of all we had been doing there that day. Several thanked Mark for his sermon which had been about the life and times of St Mark the Apostle.

No one made a move to leave the church compound, and after a while, Nick, who had gone to look around, came back and called us: 'Come and see a mega-*ugali*!' Puzzled, we followed him to where a group of women in Mothers' Union uniforms were busy over an enormous cooking pot, making *ugali* from cassava and millet, on an open fire. It was truly enormous, enough to feed the whole of Konjra!

'It must be so!' Sarah laughed, giving me a

hug. 'We are so many!'

We eventually went back to Nick's house for lunch, and even then no one was tired of praising the Lord. The singing and dancing went on long into the afternoon until some people began to lie beneath the trees for their siestas, or gradually to drift off home. When only the bishop's party and Nick's old aunt were left, it was suggested that they might be given a ride home, and we accompany them, thus seeing a little more of the countryside. Nick cheerfully agreed, and soon the car was loaded with people and bumping noisily out of the compound.

After several miles over very difficult terrain, we stopped at what appeared to be a crossroads to nowhere. 'This is where aunty gets out,' our driver announced, as the old lady turned to say goodbye to each of us. 'She has only five kilometres to walk from here.' Straight and upright, aunty soon disappeared down the overgrown path into the bush, her cheerful *leso* swaying, her gait slow and dignified as she trod barefoot out of sight. It was nearly dark by the time we had dropped the bishop, archdeacon and rural dean at their respective crossroads. Nick turned the car homewards and we seemed to fly over the pot-holes as again we joined in songs of the fellowship that came so naturally.

Nick's house looked eerie as we drove through the gates and pulled up outside.

Mosquitoes were illuminated in the headlights but there seemed no other form of life around. I got out of the car, thinking gratefully of rest and prayer after the long day, amazing with its 'God-incidences', unforgettable in its atmosphere. Suddenly, from the kitchen, sparsely lit by oil lamps, a figure appeared and came to life at the side of me. 'Sister Carol?' Jonah said as I turned to his partly illuminated face. 'The child. I have found her!'

In that second it was as if this answer to prayer was simply the perfect ending to a perfect day. 'Good!' I said fervently. I imagined how the little girl would, thanks to the project here, get the medical treatment she so badly needed. 'Where have you taken her?' I asked.

Jonah frowned. He looked straight at me as if he couldn't quite understand the question, or rather, the reasoning behind it.

'I have brought her here,' he said simply. 'She is waiting for you in the garden, under the sycamore tree.'

CHAPTER TWENTY-THREE

Suddenly, sickeningly, it all made sense. Because of our involvement with the Metropolitan Hospital, the people here assumed I was medically trained! Alice said as much as she came to my side now, offering to boil water. 'I will do this while you fetch your equipment.'

'B . . . But . . .!' I turned from their darkened faces and hopeful voices and looked back into the garden where I could see small, huddled figures. I had never felt so stupid or useless in my whole life.

Numbly, I tried to explain about both my ignorance and lack of supplies. 'We don't even have a bandage do we?' I appealed to Mark, and he, recovering from his own surprise, took me by the arm. 'Let's go and see what we *have* got,' he said. 'Meanwhile, it won't hurt to have some boiled water on hand.'

In the bedroom we made a frenzied search by candlelight and found a clean, white handkerchief, a strip of plaster, and a tiny bit of antibiotic cream, brought on the safari as an afterthought in case of insect bites. 'It's not much, but it's better than nothing,' Mark said as he picked up the nail scissors. 'Come on, darling. Let's see what we can do.'

It was as dark now as Gethsemane in that garden. The figures sat around a trestle table on which the child had been sitting, under the great tree. I could not make out their faces, but I sensed the intensity of their combined pity and revulsion as Jonah held the oil lamp aloft and the wound was exposed to sight.

'There you are, sister Carol.' Alice put the bowl of boiled water on the table and I

126

dropped the handkerchief into it. I still didn't know how I was going to touch the wound, full as it was of festering pus. Even without medical knowledge, I did know from the sweet and putrid smell that, neglected much longer, the leg, and ultimately the child too, would be a lost cause.

'Go on, darling.' Mark put his hand supportively on my shoulder as I knelt and looked up into the girl's small, resigned face, lit by the ghostly mosquito-drawing light. 'I don't want to hurt you,' I said, wishing she could speak English, or I her language. There was no response, even when I squeezed out the hankie and began, somehow, to clean the wound.

By the time I had finished, everyone was in tears except for the patient. She sat there, still silent, her mother at her side, while I did the best I could, and cursed again my own ignorance. After I had secured the wet hankie, smeared with the antibiotic, onto her leg, I put my hand on her shoulder, feeling the bones through her thin, cotton dress.

'You're a very brave girl,' I told her, and then, turning to Jonah. 'She needs to go to the hospital,' I said. 'I've done the best I can but this is a very serious wound, and I think it's badly infected.'

Jonah spoke to her mother again. She replied sounding sullen and guilty, her eyes on the ground. 'She says she has three children younger than this Patricia,' he said, 'and her husband has deserted her. She has no money for the hospital. Although she told us the child has seen a doctor, it is not true because she has no funds for medical care.'

Nick stepped forward, his hand in his pocket. 'We'll have a collection for her consultation fee,' he said as nods and words of assent came from the group. 'She will go to the hospital tomorrow, because I will drive her there.'

Patricia, still silent, looked from one to another of us, her eyes full of uncertainty and fear. I longed to be able to reassure her, and as if reading my thoughts, Mark said huskily, 'Let's pray.' So we put our hands on her head, the whole company united in our common bond of mingled hope and empathy. I felt Patricia relax against me as Mark prayed fervently for God's healing power to come upon her and save her from the infection in her body. Other voices, unsteady with emotion, joined in, claiming Patricia's healing in the name of Jesus, who said the children should come to him.

When I got back to the house, Alice washed my hands with scalding water and strong soap. 'You have been exposed to disease,' she told me as, brooking no resistance, she carefully dried my fingers. 'We do not know what these germs are, but you must be careful.'

As I went back outside, the little group

under the sycamore tree was breaking up. Suddenly struck by a thought, I hurried over to them. 'Tell Patricia's mother she must rest!' I instructed Jonah, hearing a voice of authority I scarcely recognised as my own. 'She mustn't walk to fetch water, or work in the *shamba*, for instance.'

Jonah relayed the message, and as the woman morosely nodded, Nick held up his car keys. 'I will drive them home, my sister,' he said. 'I am much afraid we are in for another night of storms.'

When he returned, we all gathered in the sitting room for our now customary family prayers. We prayed for Patricia and her family and then Alice began to ask God's help for other sufferers in Konjra.

'You know, Lord, that we have the dispensary but no medicines,' she said in a clear, fervent voice. 'You know that we need a nurse who will stay here and look after those who are ill or injured, like Patricia.'

By the time we had finished, preparing for bed with gentler choruses than usual, the rain was tipping down outside in a single, heavy sheet again. As thunder and lightning lit the sky, Dinah instinctively screeched and clung to Peter.

'Don't worry, Dinah,' Margaret said, smiling in encouragement as she passed on her way to bed. 'The Lord will take care of you. Just remember how he answered your prayers last night.'

Snug again beneath our mosquito net, Mark and I were soon trying to relax too. It had been a totally amazing day, I thought. The service and celebration, the feeling of community within the village. Most of all, that experience tonight in the garden, when my own fear and revulsion had been conquered by the instinctive compassion that knowing Jesus Christ had given me. That compassion linked me, whether I liked it or not, to this place, to St Mark's, and to Patricia, a child I could not even speak to because of our different cultures and languages. Silently I thanked God that she had been brought to our attention by the direct intervention of his word, by the authority of Jesus our living Lord, still speaking to us through the centuries and across all possible barriers.

I was so happy that with the small amount of Kenyan shillings we had collected, and Nick's car to take her, Patricia would get proper medical care at last. We could go back to Nairobi, and ultimately home to England knowing that as well as helping implement the Metropolitan Hospital chapel, we had made a real difference, even if it was only to one child's life. I fell asleep listening to the storm which seemed to have moved some distance away. But the cascading rain was still on top of the house and hammered down all night long, heavy and destructive, washing away with all the force and power of a tidal wave.

When we woke, it was to find the house almost afloat on a sea of mud. But the downpour had ceased, and I stood at the back door and watched Nick go cautiously out to his car. 'I am going to look at the roads,' he called, sounding unusually worried. 'In this weather, we sometimes have many problems.'

Mark and I had packed our bag having been told the *akamba* bus left at 9 am sharp. The plan had been to drop us in Agunja in plenty of time. Nick would then return to Konjra and pick up Patricia and her mother for the trip further east to the hospital.

'This is our last breakfast here together, my dear friends!' Alice exclaimed, as we all sat around the big table for prayers and choruses. 'We will miss you all so much when you go back to Nairobi. But don't worry, we will be back at St Stephen's ourselves in a couple of weeks, and will bring you news of Patricia and her treatment.'

Just as we were about to start the meal, passing round the saucepan of fried eggs and the soft white bread and margarine, the sound of a car door being slammed came from outside. A moment later, Nick stood in the doorway looking very grim, an unusually quiet Jonah at his side.

'Well, my brothers and sisters,' our host began regretfully. 'I am afraid to tell you that although the road to Agunja is just about

131

passable, the one I need to take to the hospital has been completely washed away. It would be madness to try to drive on it.'

'Oh no!' I recalled what Dr Gakombe had told me about a relative of his who, although he had access to several cars, had still died from diabetes. Even his expensive four-wheel-drive vehicles had been unable to get him over the rough terrain which lay between his ancestral home and the nearest doctor. I got to my feet, looking from one to another of our precious new friends. Our time here was nearly over, a little voice whispered inside me. In a couple of hours, if we were lucky, we would be back on the road to Nairobi, the problems of rural Konjra firmly behind us. But what about young Patricia and her terrible, untreated leg? It was totally unacceptable that, after what had happened last night, we should go back on our word. As if reading my anxious thoughts, Jonah suddenly stepped forward at his brother's side.

'Do not worry, sister Carol,' he said staunchly. 'God will get us where he needs us to go, and protect us on the journey. Nick's car might not be able to make it across country to the hospital, but our church taxi has no such problems. I will take Patricia to the hospital myself today—on the back of the bicycle.'

CHAPTER TWENTY-FOUR

'So we have to trust that Patricia's guardian angel will keep on looking after her,' Mark said as we later climbed off the noisy, uncomfortable bus in Nairobi. 'And let's hope Julius is here to see us safely back to Doonholm!'

I looked around the crowded street, full of careering traffic. It was 7.30 in the evening, and quite dark. We had never been in the city at night before, and I sensed Mark was as nervous as myself, remembering warnings we had been given. There was definitely no sign of Julius, and I wasn't really surprised. Not only was I not sure that he would have got the message about meeting us on Friday instead of Thursday, but also we were three and a half hours late.

We stood with our bag, feeling very self-conscious with our pale faces. I fumed as I recalled our long wait in Agunja this morning. How the *akamba* that was due at 9 am sharp had not arrived until 11.45!

'African time, my sister,' Nick had told us as he sat back and unpeeled another banana. 'We must watch the horizon and pray for that gift of the Holy Spirit which is called patience.'

Now, after nearly ten hours on the unpadded seats of the *akamba*, travelling at break-neck speed, with only one 'comfort stop' at a smelly garage latrine, I felt as if my patience had come to a definite end. I was tired, hungry, sore and scared and, to top it all, we were now stranded in the dark in this dangerous city miles from the flat where we felt safe. As I numbly and silently prayed that Julius would suddenly appear among the milling traffic, a figure came consolingly to my side. 'If you would like to take a taxi, my brother and sister, I will accompany you,' Peter offered.

'Dinah will travel home with Margaret on the *matatu*,' he went on as his wife nodded her agreement. 'She will be all right so long as there is no more thunder!'

We were so grateful for his help, and we followed him to the nearest waiting cab. 'I know you *wuzungu* must be careful,' he said as we all got inside, putting our luggage into the boot. 'And you are guests in my country, therefore the Lord tells me I must take care of you. I will be your guardian angel, eh?'

Mark and I relaxed at last, surprised at how pleased we were to see the familiar but unlovely sights of Jogoo Road soon bumping past us. 'Mind you, it is not only you people who must be careful,' Peter went on, turning from the passenger seat. 'Only last week, I too was attacked and robbed in the street. I thought it was safe, because it appeared I was in Jericho with three mamas.'

134

'Three mamas?' repeated Mark, frowning.

Peter laughed. 'Yes, three mamas in their *lesos* and headscarves were following me, and I let them catch up, unsuspecting that anything was wrong. Then suddenly they all jumped on me!'

'Oh no!'

'Yes, my sister!' Peter chortled as he remembered the incident. 'I remember praying, "O Lord, if this is how you want to take me to heaven—being attacked by three lovely mamas—then your will be done!"'

'And then?' Even the driver was agog, his face half turned to Peter as he drove.

'And then, they threw off their *lesos* and scarves and they weren't mamas at all, but big men!' Peter went on, alarm now colouring the tale. 'They were very angry when they found I had nothing but a few shillings. But praise God, they contented themselves with kicking me. They could have killed me if he had not protected me that night.'

'*Bwana asifiwe!*' I replied amid cheers, feeling positively lighthearted as we took the Doonholm turning. I couldn't wait to see the flat, and Wilomenah, and tell her all about our amazing time in Konjra. I too was very grateful for the Lord's protection on our journey home.

The next few days passed very quickly, and we became aware that we had only two weeks left in Kenya. We heard nothing from Jonah at

Konjra and St Stephen's wasn't the same without Nick and Alice. At the Metropolitan Hospital, the chapel roof was now attached and plans made, via Jemima, for regular Anglican and Roman Catholic masses to be held there. 'This is what people are asking for,' she explained as we shared a meal one night. 'It is what we have done at the government hospital for several years and it works very well.'

We continued to marvel at the enthusiasm and interest the project was still raising. Every time we visited, we found new Christians, some of them visitors, who were interested in the new chapel building.

'This is what we need at my Lutheran church,' a young, Swedish male nurse said admiringly, as we showed him the simple, pristine structure. 'But for us it would be a classroom to be used to tell the youth about Aids and HIV.'

Meanwhile, Priscilla, the chaplaincy visitor from St Paul's, wondered if the chapel could be used sometimes as a nursery. 'I have adopted two orphans,' she told us. 'My husband divorced me because I was barren, and these children needed a home. Now I must work, and they need somewhere to play and to learn to know the Lord.'

Her pride in the two small children knew no bounds, and she insisted on taking us to her home to meet them over a meal of rice and stew. Though old enough to be their grandmother, Priscilla treated the two tots with as much skill and tenderness as any mother, and showed no signs of tiring of the endless games they wanted to play.

Helped by an unmarried mother who lived in with her own child, she lived in a council house comprising one room divided into three, with a slab sink and a cooker for kitchen facilities, and beds jammed into every crevice. There was scarcely room to walk, and yet the children danced and sang there, happily joining in the Christian songs which Priscilla joyously taught them.

We were walking back from Priscilla's that night to be picked up by Julius at the hospital when an African in a turban and white robes stopped us in the street.

'*Jambo!*' he smiled, extending a hand. 'I see from your collars you are servants of our Lord Jesus Christ. My name is Emmanuel Simwa. I know the Lord, and I attend the Holy Spirit church here in Jericho.'

Mark was excited because he had been hoping to make contact with one or more of the indigenous churches. Now, by another 'God-incidence', Emmanuel had waylaid us and was soon inviting us to share in worship with them that coming Saturday.

'It will be very different to anything you have experienced before,' our friend Stanley at the Church Army advised with a twinkle in his eye. 'I shouldn't plan anything else for the rest of the day.'

Saturday came, and Julius for once was on time. He dropped us off at the hospital where we were met by Rose, who gave us three letters from home.

'You never know when they're going to arrive,' I said, tearing open the envelope with our daughter's handwriting on it. 'I'd given up asking by Thursday this week.'

'That's the nice thing about it all,' Mark replied philosophically. 'When you're not expecting anything it's twice as good when something turns up.'

I skimmed through the letters and put them in my bag to enjoy later. Emmanuel Simwa was already crossing the forecourt towards us, resplendent in robes which had bright red crosses on them.

'The men and women sit separately in our fellowship, sister,' he told me deferentially as we made our way past Jericho Market towards a hut which was fronted, like all the other buildings in the row, with garbage. 'And you must wear a headscarf and leave your shoes at the door.'

Luckily, Stanley had already told us these practicalities, so we were well prepared. We stepped through the door of a rather dilapidated building painted in green gloss. 'It used to be the CANU headquarters,' Emmanuel told us as we were shown where to sit, on separate sides of the tiny hall. 'We meet on Saturdays because we have links with the Seventh Day Adventists.'

The hall gradually filled up, with the men taking off their turbans and revealing dreadlocks. The women's headscarves bore the distinctive red cross, and the pastor, who had the longest dreadlocks and also the most solemn expression, sat behind a table and occasionally spoke, Guru like and with great passion, in Swahili.

I sat down, smelling the strange, peppery scent of overcrowding in the air. I watched, bemused, as from time to time, someone would go to the corner of the room and shout out through the window, obviously confessing their sins.

'Hallelujah!' the assembled company shouted, when the penitent, with fist and fury, cast out their sins into the waiting world beyond the barred, open window. Each time the word 'Hallelujah!' was used, a tall man standing near the front banged the drum.

'And now my friends, as you will see, we have visitors, special guests today,' Emmanuel said as the service got underway. 'I am going to ask each of them to share with us what the Lord has done for them. Hallelujah!'

The drum was banged again and again. We rose to sing and to dance. The pastor preached a fiery sermon, translated on our behalf, all about the history of the church and how in its early days it had been persecuted by white Christians. I caught Mark's eye as the tirade went on, hoping they weren't going to hold us personally responsible. But as the meeting continued, the hours of the afternoon passing like a dream, I realised we were definitely among friends. And more.

'We do not want to let you people go,' Emmanuel said after we had testified to them. 'We feel you have been sent among us for a special reason—like apostles or angels.'

'More angels,' I said thoughtfully, as Mark and I went back to the hospital to wait for Julius. It had been quite an afternoon, and I was looking forward to a restful evening. Tomorrow we were due to preach at Lavington United Methodist/ Anglican church, situated, just for a change, on the western side of the city. We had just settled down, the curtains drawn, the television flickering, when a familiar banging came at the gate below.

'It's Nick and Alice,' Mark said as he came in from unlocking all the padlocks. 'And they've brought Jonah—with news from Konjra.'

CHAPTER TWENTY-FIVE

'Here are some photographs,' Jonah said as we all exchanged greetings and settled down to talk. 'Patricia before the treatment on her leg, and after she saw the doctor.'

He described how the hazardous journey by bicycle had been successful in that Patricia had been able to have her leg expertly treated. Looking at the first pictures, I relived the scene in Nick's garden, and was relieved that the second showed some progress.

'Since that first treatment, she has had to go back to the hospital,' Jonah went on. 'The leg was very bad, as you suspected, sister Carol, and the doctor decided it must be cut.'

'Oh no!' Thinking instinctively of amputation, I caught my breath, but Nick reassured me at his brother's side.

'Patricia has to go into hospital and stay. Then they will graft new skin from the top of her leg,' he explained. 'Jonah has been telling us all about it on the way over. The only thing is, this will be expensive—about 25,000 Kenyan shillings.'

Mark and I looked at each other. 'That's what—about £250,' he said. 'Not much when you think about losing a leg.'

We agreed that Patricia must have the operation. The Lord had brought her to our attention and we knew he would supply the money that was needed. 'I'm sure St Mark's, my church in England, would agree to sponsor her long term,' I said thoughtfully, imagining the impact Patricia's story would have on my kind-hearted Black Country congregation.

141

'But in the meantime, we'll pay for the operation.'

Alice reached over and took my hand, her dark eyes very serious. 'We have also been thinking and praying about the equipping of the Konjra dispensary,' she said. 'As I explained, there is a building but no supplies, and no resident nurse.'

'We give talks to so many groups back home,' Mark said, speaking my own thoughts aloud. 'I'm sure that people will be very willing to help once they know the need is so desperate.'

After a time of worship, our visitors left, promising to keep us informed as to what was happening. Meanwhile the days whizzed by until we were in our last week in Kenya.

'Well, we know now why the Lord brought us here,' Mark said thoughtfully, as we prayed alone in the Metropolitan Hospital chapel one chilly morning. 'And as it always is with the Lord, it wasn't straightforward, and it wasn't one dimensional.'

'The chapel, and the Konjra angel,' I said quietly. 'Quite a combination!'

Having sent a cheque, via Nick, for Patricia's hospital stay and operation, I was wondering what the outcome of it all would be, wondering if, in fact, we would ever even know. All I did know was that the Lord our God had been with us, step by step of this amazing adventure. And it wasn't over yet!

'We are so sad! Sunday is your last one in Kenya,' Nick said when we popped over from the Church Army to join St Stephen's staff meeting. 'I want you to come to my place for lunch that day. I will ask one or two people, but first, the two of you must bring the word of God to us that day. You must also bring Wilomenah and Julius, those people the Lord gave to help you. We will all travel together.'

'You don't mean to Konjra, Nick?' I asked, my heart stopping in spite of myself. Our companion threw back his head and bellowed with laughter.

'No, otherwise Sunday would become Monday, and then another week would go by and you would miss your flight!' he exclaimed. 'I was speaking, my sister, of our home in Nairobi, the house the church has given me on loan.'

Early on the Sunday morning, Julius arrived with Wilomenah to take us to church. He was early again, and she told us in no uncertain terms that he was obeying orders—hers.

'I tell him we cannot be even one minute late for this special day,' she explained as we got cheerfully into the old vehicle. 'I prayed to the Lord to make him early, and you see, he has not let me down.'

Both cook and driver were wearing their Sunday best clothes, and as we set out to make our way to Jogoo Road, the atmosphere was warm and festive. Mark and I had been booked to preach at both services, he at the Swahili and me at the English service. It was good to hear the buzz of recognition when I got up into the pulpit, to feel the accumulation of all those weeks since we came here as strangers. I preached on Jesus' encounter with the woman at the well, and King Solomon's encounter with the Queen of Sheba, speaking of different cultures and the relationship between men and women, and how different it was in Kenya to what we had grown accustomed to in the West.

Afterwards, one of the lay readers who joined us in the vestry asked if I had a copy of the sermon. He would like to use the same text when he preached at a conference soon. I handed over my one and only copy without a second thought, realising how different the criteria were even of ministry here in Kenya.

'And now my brother Mark will preach in Swahili!' Nick later joked to the second, enormous congregation. Mark got to his feet amid claps and was borne to the high pulpit on a wave of singing, his interpreter close by his side.

'There were three people in that pulpit today, my friend,' the archdeacon twinkled as we later congregated outside in our processional circle. 'You, the interpreter, and the Holy Spirit.'

'Amen!' Nick rejoined, and several people agreed that Mark's sermon, his last at

St Stephen's, had certainly been one to remember.

'The Mothers' Union are waiting for you, my sister,' I was told a few minutes later, and so I hurried back into the church where a whole group of the blue-clad ladies, led by Esther, their enrolling member, sat in the front pew.

'We have gifts for you before we say goodbye,' Esther explained, drawing both Mark and myself into the centre of the group. 'But first, we must have speeches to express what it has meant to have you with us, and your wonderful husband.'

Nodding pointedly to the men who were milling curiously around, she went on to explain how our way of doing things together had been a source of wonder and inspiration to their Mothers' Union group.

'Mark has come to the meetings with you, something our men never do. He has shown us it is possible for a man and a woman to share equally in the work of the Lord.'

'You—you have taught us a lot too,' I said, amid the hugs and cheers. 'In our country having the meeting is sometimes more important than knowing the Lord. We're going to tell them about your African time, and see if we can't take some of it back with us.'

Catching a glimpse of Nick and his family by the main doors, we regretfully began to excuse ourselves. 'Sorry, but we have to go. We're going to Reverend Nick's for lunch.'

The combined Mothers' Union looked up at us in surprise. 'So are we, my sister,' Esther replied, beaming in pleasure. 'We are all coming to lunch, but we thought we would like to see you alone first.'

The lunch party, one of many farewell meals, lasted from 12.30, when we arrived at Nick's with Julius and Wilomenah, until 7 pm. Nick's church house was not as picturesque or as scenically set as his ancestral home in Konjra, but it was comfortable, the place where his family of six children had grown up. The happy company spilled out through the ground-floor rooms and into the garden where trestle tables were laid. The food was simple but substantial, the traditional African fare of stew, chapatis, chicken and fruit and *irio*, made of peas, potatoes and maize, which we had grown used to. People sang and talked and praised God, sharing their faith as easily and naturally as they shared their fellowship. As lunch became afternoon tea, people drifted away and others wandered in, bringing hugs and good wishes, songs and prayers.

Before we left, reluctantly insisting that we must go before dark, each of our companions stood up in turn and at Nick's invitation introduced themselves to the assembled company, giving their testimony before expressing their gratitude and pleasure for all we shared as children of the same heavenly

Father. Several times, Mark and I were called to respond, and I wondered where all the words and the energy were coming from. We all seemed to be on fire, lit quietly but certainly from within. We stood and sang choruses, swaying and dancing, putting the familiar actions to the songs, and tears ran down our faces as we sang the old Moody and Sankey hymns that were so popular here and brought back happy memories of our own childhood days in Sunday school.

Finally we were allowed to leave, although Nick stressed that anyone who wished could stay on. We began to say our individual goodbyes. To Sheila, the lady who looked after the street children. To Abida, who danced but spoke no English. To Dinah and Peter, with whom we had shared so much in Konjra.

Eventually we got into the car. 'Bye,' I called through the window. 'Thank you so m . . .'

I got no further because Nick, shaking our hands, was already reminding Mark of another date. 'We will all be meeting up again on Wednesday, in church,' he said as the Mothers' Union and others gathered round, smiling and nodding. 'The archdeacon has asked me to remind you people to be there at six.'

'Oh?' Mark and I looked from him to each other in surprise. It was the first we had heard of it!

'Of course!' Nick exclaimed, slapping Julius

on the shoulder as he jerked the car into gear. 'It is very important that we see you—we still have to say goodbye.'

CHAPTER TWENTY-SIX

'I have slept at the hospital so that I may not be late,' Julius explained amid cheers and laughter. He had arrived to take us to the airport at precisely 6 am, having taken to heart Wilomenah's warning all week. To be on the safe side, she had also arranged for her husband, George, to come along in his car and he had brought four of their five children. 'We will all come and wave to you when you get on the aeroplane to London,' she had said. 'We will be sad, but I know that God is going to bring you back to Kenya one day.'

During our times of quiet in the flat, Wilomenah had told us about the opportunities here for anyone who had enough capital to buy a plot of land. 'You could build a home, the materials are close by,' she said, eyes sparkling as she warmed to her subject. 'And then I or one of my girls could come and work for you.'

We had now grown so used to this other world of hardship and poverty, faith and miracles that part of me responded very forcefully to the suggestion of making a home there. And yet, what did we really have to offer? We were like people from another planet, a planet which was advanced and sophisticated and yet jaded and degenerate. All we could really do was what we had done— leave behind as many of our material goods as we could, knowing they would be used and valued here. When we got home, we hoped, somehow, to create links so that Christians in both societies would gain and learn from each other.

As we drove along the unusually quiet road to the airport with Julius, I really felt we had come full circle. My thoughts went back to the culture shock and anxiety of my first trip in his old car—was it really only three months ago? So much had happened since—the setting up of the hospital chapel where, yesterday, we had said goodbye to Jemima and our friends and colleagues. We hoped and prayed that the work would go on and intensify as the hospital grew to its full potential of 200 beds. I thought of St Stephen's, and the final goodbyes that were said on Wednesday when the church council got together in the hall with the Mothers' Union and overwhelmed us with gifts and food and speeches. We had been humbled by their love, their simple enjoyment of the time we had spent together. That, too, had been part of God's plan that had brought me to Africa, to share in and benefit from that wonderful worship.

149

'You're very quiet,' Mark said as we turned into the airport.

I looked at him and smiled, thinking of the other miraculous thing which had happened through our being here. 'I'm just wondering if Jonah will make it to see us off,' I said. 'Nick did say he might be able to bring him to the airport if last night's *akamba* was on time.'

It would be so good, I thought, to have news of Richard, our sponsor child, and Patricia, to take back with us. But there was no sign of the project leader, and as we settled into the comfortable seats in the airport lobby and the time began to pass, I realised it had been too optimistic of me to expect him to travel such a distance.

All too soon, it was time to move into the departure lounge.

'*Kwaheri*, my sister,' Wilomenah enfolded me in her warm arms.

'*Kwaheri*, Wilomenah. Thank you for taking care of us.'

'And thank you, Julius. You are the best driver in the world.'

'Yes,' Mark put in, shaking Julius' hand. 'Even when your car breaks down.'

We said goodbye to George, and the children, and then walked slowly away, feeling bereft as we left their well-known figures standing near the door. It was like bidding farewell to beloved family members, and we realised just how close we had become, and

150

how deep were the bonds between us. It seemed impossible that in a few hours we would be back in England, with all the mod cons we had taken for granted, and missed, and finally forgotten about. As the plane took off an hour later, I looked around at my fellow passengers, seeing more European faces than I had seen in the whole of the past three months.

'People back home will listen for three minutes when you tell them what it's like out here,' Stanley at the Church Army had warned us affectionately when we went to say goodbye. 'Then they'll start to get a glassy-eyed look and change the subject. Nobody wants to be made to feel guilty.'

Is that what we had to do in order to forge those links—to get some real and lasting financial assistance in places like Konjra? I hoped not. All I knew was I had to tell the story, and leave people's response to their own hearts and the workings of the Holy Spirit.

Meanwhile there were real joys to be anticipated, like seeing Sarah, Andy and Edmund again. Like sleeping in our own bed without a mosquito net, like being able to walk in comparative safety out of doors, and to drive on what would surely seem heavenly safe roads again. In addition, we knew there were people waiting for us. Letters not only from the family, but from members of our congregations spoke of counting the days, and we knew we were assured of a welcome, not only at St Mark's, but at Mark's Methodist churches.

Thinking of that voice inside me saying, 'Go to Africa', I felt a sense of relief and gratitude that once I had said, 'Yes', God had so miraculously made it all possible. There was a new sense of peace inside me, a new knowledge that part of his plan for my life, and the lives of others, had been fulfilled.

We arrived at Heathrow on that Saturday evening feeling tired but elated. I walked through the British passport control alone, parting with Mark while he waited in a long queue with his American passport. Looking round, seeing all the white faces and the rushing bodies, dressed in what seemed to me revealing and unflattering clothes, I felt momentarily dazed. It was like coming back from outer space, and I wondered if the early astronauts had felt this way.

Finally, unable to stand it any longer, I went down the escalator to begin to reclaim our baggage, and Mark joined me later. Eventually we emerged, blinking, out of the arrivals lounge, and there Sarah, Andy and Edmund were, waiting for us, pretending to hide, like the children they still were.

It was simply wonderful to see and touch them again, to hear their news as we made our way to the car park where our own car, unseen for three months, waited for us. As we drove along in comparative comfort and safety, it really seemed like coming out of a dream. I wondered, not for the first time, how we would be able to tell our story and do it full justice, and inwardly I prayed that God would be as close to us here as he had been in our daily life these past few months in Kenya. Otherwise we would have no alternative. We would simply have to go back!

CHAPTER TWENTY-SEVEN

Three weeks later, the letters arrived. They had been three busy weeks of adjustments on all sides. We had forgotten that our churches and even the family had had time to get used to being without us.

We stared around ordinary, West Midlands Pensnett, blooming in summer foliage. It was beautiful and green and clean compared to eastern Nairobi. We looked at our ordinary home and the homes of our friends and neighbours and we saw that we were all very, very rich, with carpets and vacuum cleaners, washing machines, running water and electricity that could be relied upon.

We gloried in the simple things money couldn't buy, like the ecstatic, long-winded welcome from our pets, Becky and Jacob. But even as we looked at them, we couldn't help reminding ourselves how lucky they were too. Dogs and cats had little chance in the environment where we had been, where people struggled to be fed.

And so the letters arrived at exactly the right time. A letter from Jonah at Konjra, enclosing photographs of Richard, and Patricia smiling as she sat outside St Mark's, her bandaged left leg extended, a pair of shoes on her feet. Jonah's letter thanked us for the cheque and explained the progress which had been made because of it. Patricia was out of hospital now, he said, and her skin graft was healing nicely. She was staying with the social worker from the project, who was making sure she had proper care.

The other letter, to my delight and astonishment, was from Patricia herself—though it had been written on her behalf by Jonah. 'Dear Mother,' it began, and as I read it I wept as I learnt for the first time something of the inner person—the frightened child in the garden that dark night. 'Patricia says it was a miracle that you sent a message that you wanted to see her after you met her on the road. She says she cannot forget the way you struggled with her leg, because that was when her treatment began. She says her father had told her that her leg would have to be cut off, and so she had lost all hope.

'She thanks God, and she wants you to know that she loves the Lord Jesus. She is a pupil now at St Mark's Primary School, Konjra, where she prays for you and brother Mark.'

'The sponsorship application is coming up at the PCC next week,' I told Mark excitedly. 'If I show them this letter and the new photos, I'm sure they will be even keener to help.'

The possibility of providing more care and resources for the dispensary was at the centre of our prayers. We received letters from Alice and Nick, saying they were praying for it too, and asking for whatever aid we could find.

'We need a proper project,' Mark said as we collected our Kenyan slides from the local chemist's the following week. 'Something that will get people's interest and sympathy.'

'Project Patricia!' I exclaimed. 'We tell the story and we get some leaflets printed, asking for donations. Then we can send supplies and cash.'

'What they really need is a nurse on duty,' Mark replied. 'Someone skilled who can be paid a regular salary.'

I nodded. 'First, we need to keep the link going,' I said. 'Then, if possible, for someone to go over there again—see what's happening with their own eyes, and report back to the people over here.'

We worked and prayed and I preached a sermon which made several members of my congregation weep. Ancrum Evans, hearing the story when we met to update him on the progress of the hospital, was both moved and astonished that his sponsorship had taken us so far into uncharted territory.

The PCC gladly accepted the idea of sponsoring Patricia Auma, and the project to equip the dispensary got under way as we gave our slide shows and talks. Wherever we went with our story, Christians were stirred into action, and within the first few weeks we raised a staggering £500, as well as many promises of medical supplies. Gradually, the Kenyan wicker basket, a present from St Stephen's Mothers' Union which we placed in St Mark's Lady chapel, began to fill with bandages, antiseptic and plasters.

Then one night, one of our church members, a man who had always lovingly supported my ministry, asked to see me in private. 'My daughter, Claire, would like to come and talk to you, Carol,' he said, looking excited. 'She's got a proposition she wants to put to you.'

Claire was a lovely girl of twenty-one, in her second year at the University of Cardiff, studying nursing. I had known her for several years as a chorister.

When Claire came into our living room, there was something about her, a glow I couldn't quite explain. 'Dad sent me your leaflet about Patricia,' she said, 'and it made me think. You see, next year, as part of my training, I have to do a project which involves study, travel and practical work. It's only initially for a month, but . . .'

'But?' I stared, wondering what all this had to do with me.

Young Claire sighed, and bit her lip. She looked out of the window as if towards a far horizon. 'Well, you see, Reverend Carol,' she said. 'You might think this sounds silly, but I keep hearing a voice inside me saying, "Go to Africa!"'